OXFORD STUDENT TEXTS

Series Editor: Victor Lee

Chaucer: The Miller's Tale

Geoffrey Chaucer

The Miller's Tale

Edited by
Peter Mack and Chris Walton

Oxford University Press

OXFORD
UNIVERSITY PRESS

Great Clarendon Street, Oxford OX2 6DP

Oxford University Press is a department of the University of Oxford.
It furthers the University's objective of excellence in research, scholarship,
and education by publishing worldwide in

Oxford   New York

Auckland   Cape Town   Dar es Salaam   Hong Kong   Karachi
Kuala Lumpur   Madrid   Melbourne   Mexico City   Nairobi
New Delhi   Shanghai   Taipei   Toronto

With offices in

Argentina   Austria   Brazil   Chile   Czech Republic   France   Greece
Guatemala   Hungary   Italy   Japan   South Korea   Poland   Portugal
Singapore   Switzerland   Thailand   Turkey   Ukraine   Vietnam

Oxford is a registered trade mark of Oxford University Press
in the UK and in certain other countries

British Library Cataloguing in Publication Data
Data available

ISBN: 978-0-19-832577-2

5 7 9 10 8 6 4

Typeset in Goudy Old Style MT
by Palimpsest Book Production Limited, Grangemouth, Stirlingshire

Printed in Great Britain by CPI Group (UK) Ltd, Croydon, CR0 4YY

The publishers would like to thank the following for permission to reproduce photographs:
px: Mary Evans Picture Library; p3: Ludovic Maisant/Corbis; p8: Mary Evans Picture Library
(both); p102: Mary Evans Picture Library; p115 both: Corbis; p134: Visual Arts Library
Library/Alamy.

Artwork is by Jason Lewis.

Contents

Acknowledgements

Peter Mack would like to acknowledge the help he received in compiling the Notes from the critical works and editions listed in Further Reading, and from his colleagues, Gloria Cigman and Bill Whitehead. He is grateful to Robert Burchfield for his comments on the Note on Chaucer's English. Chris Walton would like to thank his previous A-level students for their helpful comments on the first edition of this text, Erica Holley for valuable historical resources and Barbara Mitchell for providing critical material. Both authors would like to thank Victor Lee, Jan Doorly, Karen Hemingway, and Lucy Hooper for their constructive criticism and advice. The text is taken from *The Riverside Chaucer*, Third Edition, edited by Larry D. Benson, copyright © 1987 by Houghton Mifflin Company.

Editors

Dr Victor Lee, the series editor, read English at University College, Cardiff. He was later awarded his doctorate at the University of Oxford. He has taught at secondary and tertiary level, working at the Open University for 27 years. Victor Lee's experience as an examiner is very wide. He has been, for example, a Chief Examiner in English A-level for three different boards, stretching over a period of more than 30 years.

Professor Peter Mack read English at St Peter's College, Oxford and went on to gain an MPhil and PhD in Renaissance Studies from the Warburg Institute, University of London. He has examined English at GCSE and A level as well as for the International Baccalaureate. He has been Editor of the journal, *Rhetorica* and Head of the English Department at the University of Warwick, where he has taught Medieval English Studies since 1979. His books include *Renaissance Argument* (1993), *Renaissance Rhetoric* (1994) and *Elizabethan Rhetoric* (2002).

Chris Walton read English Literature and Philosophy at Leeds University and gained an MPhil in classroom research from Bath University. He has taught A-level English and English Literature for over 30 years and has written modular syllabuses in the subjects. He has published revision and study guides for GCSE and A level. After working as a headteacher, he is currently developing reforms in the 14–19 curriculum for Swindon and he is also a registered School Improvement Partner in the secondary sector.

Foreword

Oxford Student Texts are specifically aimed at presenting poetry and drama to an audience studying English literature at an advanced level. Each text is designed as an integrated whole consisting of four main parts. The first part sets the scene by discussing the context in which the work was written. The most important part of the book is the poetry or play itself, and it is suggested that the student reads this first without consulting the Notes or other secondary sources. To encourage students to follow this advice, the Notes are placed together after the text, not alongside it. Where help is needed, the Notes and Interpretations sections provide it.

The Notes perform two functions. First, they provide information and explain allusions. Second (this is where they differ from most texts at this level), they often raise questions of central concern to the interpretation of the poetry or play being dealt with, particularly in the general note placed at the beginning of each set of notes.

The fourth part, the Interpretations section, deals with major issues of response to the particular selection of poetry or drama. One of the major aims of this part of the text is to emphasize that there is no one right answer to interpretation, but a series of approaches. Readers are given guidance as to what counts as evidence, but in the end left to make up their own minds as to which are the most suitable interpretations, or to add their own.

In these revised editions, the Interpretations section now addresses a wider range of issues. There is a more detailed treatment of context and critical history, for example. The section contains a number of activity-discussion sequences, although it must be stressed that these are optional. Significant issues about the poetry or play are raised, and readers are invited to tackle activities before proceeding to the discussion section, where possible responses to the questions raised are considered. Their main function is to engage readers actively in the ideas of the text.

At the end of each text there is also a list of Essay Questions. Whereas the activity-discussion sequences are aimed at increasing understanding of the literary work itself, these tasks are intended to help explore ideas about the poetry or play after the student has completed the reading of the work and the studying of the Notes and Interpretations. These tasks are particularly helpful for coursework projects or in preparing for an examination.

Victor Lee *Series Editor*

CHAUCER.

A woodcut based on a portrait miniature of Chaucer from the
Ellesmere manuscript of *The Canterbury Tales*. The manuscript was
copied and illustrated a few years after Chaucer's death.

Chaucer's *Miller's Tale* in Context

Conditions of writing

At the time Chaucer (c.1343–1400) wrote and for two centuries afterwards, it was impossible to make a living by writing alone. In order to support themselves writers needed other jobs (Chaucer worked as a diplomat and a civil servant; some other writers worked as priests) and patronage, which usually took the form of gifts of money in return for the dedication of a poem or book, or the gift of a manuscript copy. The only people with the financial resources to provide patronage were the King, the great barons of the realm and, increasingly in the fourteenth and fifteenth centuries, wealthy London merchants.

Chaucer was the son of a London wine merchant, in whose house he would have learned to read and write English and French (and he may have learned Italian from his father's business associates). At school he learned Latin (which was the language of learning and of much international communication) and rhetoric (the art of speaking and writing effectively). He would also have read widely in Latin poetry. In 1357, at the age of about 14, Chaucer went to be a page in the household of Elizabeth, Countess of Ulster and Prince Lionel, King Edward III's second son, and in 1359 he was sent to France as a squire in the English army. So Chaucer combined a London mercantile origin and basic education with the training and early manhood experiences of a courtier.

In the fourteenth century it was relatively expensive to obtain a manuscript (and, of course manuscripts were the only kind of books before the invention of printing around 1465). Usually you had to borrow a copy of the work you wanted, buy parchment and ink, and hire a scribe to copy it out for you; some booksellers hired scribes to make ready-to-buy copies of books they thought would sell, but the cost of this service was higher.

I

Few people knew how to read or had the leisure to do so. In great courts a poet might read from his book to the nobles, their feudal supporters and their servants. The feudal system of land tenure meant that great lords held their lands in return for military service to and attendance on the King. In the same way, lesser feudal lords would owe service to their superiors and expect service and attendance from the knights and squires dependent on them. Merchant families who were sufficiently wealthy to afford books for leisure (some such families would have owned books only for business, for example, law books or books connected with a trade, or religious books, for the important purpose of saving their souls) may have imitated courtly practice with after-meal readings of poetry to the whole family, or family members may have read to themselves.

Because the main sources of patronage were aristocratic, non-religious literature tends to employ aristocratic forms, like the romance, and to uphold aristocratic values. Since the great merchants aspired to (and sometimes did) join the aristocracy they would have followed aristocratic tastes, but they (and especially lesser merchants) may have been more willing to entertain mockery or criticism of, for example, aristocratic complacency and idleness. Although merchants, like Chaucer's father, made much of their money from paid service to the King and nobles, their position was ultimately reliant on the financial profits they could make. They were both partly independent of the state and also more reliant than aristocrats on their own ability to respond quickly to the challenges and opportunities of the international market.

There is some manuscript and historical evidence that whereas Chaucer's earlier poems, such as *The Book of the Duchess* and *Troilus and Criseyde*, were directed to royal or aristocratic patrons, *The Canterbury Tales*, which he wrote towards the end of his career and left incomplete at his death, was intended for a London business audience. This would have been a good reason for adding representatives of various trades to the pilgrims, as he does in *The General Prologue*. For a courtly audience it would

This medieval stained glass window from Canterbury Cathedral shows pilgrims on their way to the cathedral

have seemed strange to write about a large group of people that included only one knight and his squire.

The Miller and the Knight

After choosing the Knight to tell the first tale through the drawing of lots, the Host intends that the next tale should be told by the Monk, a religious pilgrim, whose hobbies suggest that he is also of high birth, but the drunken Miller interrupts in a loud voice, insisting on telling his tale first. The image of hierarchical order thus disrupted is confirmed when the Reeve starts to quarrel with the Miller, anticipating that the Miller's story about a carpenter who is cuckolded will be an attack on him.

As a *fabliau* (see Notes, pp. 49–50 and Interpretations, pp. 106–9) *The Miller's Tale* inverts the values of the Knight's romance. Where the romance, dealing with noble characters, assumes an idealistic view of people and love, the *fabliau*, usually concerned with the lower classes, assumes that people's principal motivating forces are greed and sexual desire. *The Miller's Tale* has been considered a deliberately tailored answer to *The Knight's Tale* because of the similarities in plot structure (Alison, like Arcite, is confronted with a choice between two young men who admire her), because of an element of parody (see below) and because both tales raise (though in very different ways) the issue of divine influence on human affairs.

So *The Miller's Tale* can be considered a disruption of the host's orderly plan and an assertion of a more vulgar and materialistic view of life.

Adapting the *fabliau*

Chaucer was the first to write *fabliaux* in English and he only gave this genre to lower-class pilgrims (such as the Miller, the Reeve, the Shipman, and the Merchant). However, the existing manuscripts containing *fabliaux* and the conditions in which literature was preserved and consumed suggest that the *fabliau* was not a form of popular literature, but a genre intended for better-off readers. It has been pointed out that the victims of deception in *fabliaux* are always members of the lower classes who aspire to a higher status. In other words, the *fabliau* genre, at least in its French and Dutch forms, could be thought of as confirming aristocratic prejudices about the essentially animalistic behaviour of the churls. But Chaucer radically changed the *fabliau* genre. In his stories he takes the endings from *fabliaux* he has read, but writes introductions to the participants and their world, making what happens to them more meaningful for his audience. His *fabliaux* are about characters whereas earlier *fabliaux* dealt only in types. The yoking of *fabliau* events with imagined characters can provoke mixed and questioning responses.

In *The Miller's Tale*, vocabulary and ideas, which in romances belong to noble lovers, are attributed with comic effect to lower-class characters. So we are told that Nicholas says he will die for love of Alison (in courtly fashion) at the same time as he grabs her hard by the thighs (which would be normal in *fabliau*). Nicholas's use of this language parodies the way it was used by Palemon and Arcite in *The Knight's Tale*. We are told of the accomplishments of Absolon, of his devotion to Alison and of the gifts he brings (as we would be in a romance), but his skills, behaviour and gifts belong to his own bourgeois world and so seem comically inappropriate to romance, as well as being touchingly inappropriate to Alison, who is more receptive to the direct approach.

At the same time Chaucer retains and even enhances the impact of the *fabliau* plot as each of the men is humiliated. In Chaucer's hands this humiliation seems meaningful as well as amusing as the men are punished not just as examples of their type (for example, the old husband, the squeamish youth) but also for their chosen actions in aspiring to be holier, cleverer or nobler than their origins dictate. In another way, then, this *fabliau*

5

can be seen as socially conservative, reinforcing the distinctions between classes and punishing those who aspire to improve themselves.

Reality and imagination

Just as the Knight celebrated in detail the equipment and ceremony of courtly life in his tale, so the Miller presents an intensely real picture of the carpenter's house and West Oxford life in the fourteenth century. To describe the blacksmith's shop, the contents of the student's bedroom, the women at the services in the Abbey and the hole in the wall for the cat is to extend the subject-matter of literature and to assert the significance of ordinary life in relation to the courtly subjects more usual in fourteenth-century poetry.

Within this intensely realized world, Chaucer depicts an extraordinary fantasy in which the student, Nicholas persuades the carpenter, John to think of himself as a second Noah and to prepare tubs in his roof rafters with which to survive an impending flood, which will supposedly destroy the rest of the world. Absolon fantasizes himself as a noble lover and Alison as a delicate lady. These fantasies, which exploit the tradition of the *fabliau*, prompt mirth and delight in the audience. But Chaucer's combination of a real, physical world in which people act on their desires with an imaginative understanding of these people's dreams (absurd as they are) gives his audience an insight into the mingled fabric of human life. In its expressive power Chaucer's *fabliau* equals or even surpasses the better-established psychological insights of a great medieval romance. Chaucer may have been encouraged in his creative combination of genres and styles by the possibilities offered by the mercantile audience, partly sceptical of the pretensions of the aristocracy and partly anxious to defend their own positions in a newly expanded élite against the aspirations of tradesmen and peasants.

The Miller and the Reeve: two marginal illustrations from the Ellesmere manuscript. Compare the illustration of the Miller with the description on p9.

8

The Miller's Tale

The Miller's portrait:
General Prologue

545   The MILLERE was a stout carl for the nones;
Ful byg he was of brawn, and eek of bones.
That proved wel, for over al ther he cam,
At wrastlynge he wolde have alwey the ram.
He was short-sholdred, brood, a thikke knarre;
550   Ther was no dore that he nolde heve of harre,
Or breke it at a rennyng with his heed.
His berd as any sowe or fox was reed,
And therto brood, as though it were a spade.
Upon the cop right of his nose he hade
555   A werte, and theron stood a toft of herys,
Reed as the brustles of a sowes erys;
His nosethirles blake were and wyde.
A swerd and a bokeler bar he by his syde.
His mouth as greet was as a greet forneys.
560   He was a janglere and a goliardeys,
And that was moost of synne and harlotries.
Wel koude he stelen corn and tollen thries;
And yet he hadde a thombe of gold, pardee.
A whit cote and a blew hood wered he.
565   A baggepipe wel koude he blowe and sowne,
And therwithal he broghte us out of towne.

The Miller's Prologue

Heere folwen the wordes bitwene the Hoost and the Millere.

Whan that the Knyght had thus his tale ytoold,
In al the route nas ther yong ne oold
That he ne seyde it was a noble storie
And worthy for to drawen to memorie,
5   And namely the gentils everichon.
Oure Hooste lough and swoor, 'So moot I gon,
This gooth aright; unbokeled is the male.
Lat se now who shal telle another tale;
For trewely the game is wel bigonne.
10 Now telleth ye, sir Monk, if that ye konne,
Somwhat to quite with the Knyghtes tale.'
The Millere, that for dronken was al pale,
So that unnethe upon his hors he sat,
He nolde avalen neither hood ne hat,
15 Ne abyde no man for his curteisie,
But in Pilates voys he gan to crie,
And swoor, 'By armes, and by blood and bones,
I kan a noble tale for the nones,
With which I wol now quite the Knyghtes tale.'
20 Oure Hooste saugh that he was dronke of ale,
And seyde, 'Abyd, Robyn, my leeve brother;
Som bettre man shal telle us first another.
Abyd, and lat us werken thriftily.'
'By Goddes soule,' quod he, 'that wol nat I;
25 For I wol speke or elles go my wey.'
Oure Hoost answerde, 'Tel on, a devel wey!
Thou art a fool; thy wit is overcome.'
'Now herkneth,' quod the Millere, 'alle and some!
But first I make a protestacioun

30 That I am dronke; I knowe it by my soun.
And therfore if that I mysspeke or seye,
Wyte it the ale of Southwerk, I you preye.
For I wol telle a legende and a lyf
Bothe of a carpenter and of his wyf,
35 How that a clerk hath set the wrightes cappe.'
　　The Reve answerde and seyde, 'Stynt thy clappe!
Lat be thy lewed dronken harlotrye.
It is a synne and eek a greet folye
To apeyren any man, or hym defame,
40 And eek to bryngen wyves in swich fame.
Thou mayst ynogh of othere thynges seyn.'
　　This dronke Millere spak ful soone ageyn
And seyde, 'Leve brother Osewold,
Who hath no wyf, he is no cokewold.
45 But I sey nat therfore that thou art oon;
Ther been ful goode wyves many oon,
And evere a thousand goode ayeyns oon badde.
That knowestow wel thyself, but if thou madde.
Why artow angry with my tale now?
50 I have a wyf, pardee, as wel as thow;
Yet nolde I, for the oxen in my plogh,
Take upon me moore than ynogh,
As demen of myself that I were oon;
I wol bileve wel that I am noon.
55 An housbonde shal nat been inquisityf
Of Goddes pryvetee, nor of his wyf.
So he may fynde Goddes foyson there,
Of the remenant nedeth nat enquere.'
　　What sholde I moore seyn, but this Millere
60 He nolde his wordes for no man forbere,
But tolde his cherles tale in his manere.
M'athynketh that I shal reherce it heere.
And therfore every gentil wight I preye,

For Goddes love, demeth nat that I seye
65 Of yvel entente, but for I moot reherce
Hir tales alle, be they bettre or werse,
Or elles falsen som of my mateere.
And therfore, whoso list it nat yheere,
Turne over the leef and chese another tale;
70 For he shal fynde ynowe, grete and smale,
Of storial thyng that toucheth gentillesse,
And eek moralitee and hoolynesse.
Blameth nat me if that ye chese amys.
The Millere is a cherl; ye knowe wel this.
75 So was the Reve eek and othere mo,
And harlotrie they tolden bothe two.
Avyseth yow, and put me out of blame;
And eek men shal nat maken ernest of game.

The Miller's Tale

Heere bigynneth the Millere his tale.

     Whilom ther was dwellynge at Oxenford
80 A riche gnof, that gestes heeld to bord,
And of his craft he was a carpenter.
With hym ther was dwellynge a poure scoler,
Hadde lerned art, but al his fantasye
Was turned for to lerne astrologye,
85 And koude a certeyn of conclusiouns,
To demen by interrogaciouns,
If that men asked hym, in certein houres
Whan that men sholde have droghte or elles shoures,
Or if men asked hym what sholde bifalle
90 Of every thyng; I may nat rekene hem alle.
    This clerk was cleped hende Nicholas.
Of deerne love he koude and of solas;
And therto he was sleigh and ful privee,
And lyk a mayden meke for to see.
95 A chambre hadde he in that hostelrye
Allone, withouten any compaignye,
Ful fetisly ydight with herbes swoote;
And he hymself as sweete as is the roote
Of lycorys or any cetewale.
100 His Almageste, and bookes grete and smale,
His astrelabie, longynge for his art,
His augrym stones layen faire apart,
On shelves couched at his beddes heed;
His presse ycovered with a faldyng reed;
105 And al above ther lay a gay sautrie,
On which he made a-nyghtes melodie
So swetely that all the chambre rong;
And *Angelus ad virginem* he song;

And after that he song the Kynges Noote.
110   Ful often blessed was his myrie throte.
And thus this sweete clerk his tyme spente
After his freendes fyndyng and his rente.
      This carpenter hadde wedded newe a wyf,
Which that he lovede moore than his lyf;
115   Of eighteteene yeer she was of age.
Jalous he was, and heeld hire narwe in cage,
For she was wylde and yong, and he was old
And demed hymself been lik a cokewold.
He knew nat Catoun, for his wit was rude,
120   That bad man sholde wedde his simylitude.
Men sholde wedden after hire estaat,
For youthe and elde is often at debaat.
But sith that he was fallen in the snare,
He moste endure, as oother folk, his care.
125   Fair was this yonge wyf, and therwithal
As any wezele hir body gent and smal.
A ceynt she werede, barred al of silk,
A barmclooth as whit as morne milk
Upon hir lendes, ful of many a goore.
130   Whit was hir smok, and broyden al bifoore
And eek bihynde, on hir coler aboute,
Of col-blak silk, withinne and eek withoute.
The tapes of hir white voluper
Were of the same suyte of hir coler;
135   Hir filet brood of silk, and set ful hye.
And sikerly she hadde a likerous ye;
Ful smale ypulled were hire browes two,
And tho were bent and blake as any sloo.
She was ful moore blisful on to see
140   Than is the newe pere-jonette tree,
And softer than the wolle is of a wether.
And by hir girdel heeng a purs of lether,

Tasseled with silk and perled with latoun.
In al this world, to seken up and doun,
145 There nys no man so wys that koude thenche
So gay a popelote or swich a wenche.
Ful brighter was the shynyng of hir hewe
Than in the Tour the noble yforged newe.
But of hir song, it was as loude and yerne
150 As any swalwe sittynge on a berne.
Therto she koude skippe and make game,
As any kyde or calf folwynge his dame.
Hir mouth was sweete as bragot or the meeth,
Or hoord of apples leyd in hey or heeth.
155 Wynsynge she was, as is a joly colt,
Long as a mast, and upright as a bolt.
A brooch she baar upon hir lowe coler,
As brood as is the boos of a bokeler.
Hir shoes were laced on hir legges hye.
160 She was a prymerole, a piggesnye,
For any lord to leggen in his bedde,
Or yet for any good yeman to wedde.

   Now, sire, and eft, sire, so bifel the cas
That on a day this hende Nicholas
165 Fil with this yonge wyf to rage and pleye,
Whil that hir housbonde was at Oseneye,
As clerkes ben ful subtile and ful queynte;
And prively he caughte hire by the queynte,
And seyde, 'Ywis, but if ich have my wille,
170 For deerne love of thee, lemman, I spille.'
And heeld hire harde by the haunchebones,
And seyde, 'Lemman, love me al atones,
Or I wol dyen, also God me save!'
And she sproong as a colt dooth in the trave,
175 And with hir heed she wryed faste awey,
And seyde, 'I wol nat kisse thee, by my fey!

Why, lat be!' quod she. 'Lat be, Nicholas,
Or I wol crie "out, harrow" and "allas"!
Do wey youre handes, for youre curteisye!'
180   This Nicholas gan mercy for to crye,
And spak so faire, and profred him so faste,
That she hir love hym graunted atte laste,
And swoor hir ooth, by Seint Thomas of Kent,
That she wol been at his comandement,
185   Whan that she may hir leyser wel espie.
'Myn housbonde is so ful of jalousie
That but ye wayte wel and been privee,
I woot right wel I nam but deed,' quod she.
'Ye moste been ful deerne, as in this cas.'
190   'Nay, therof care thee noght,' quod Nicholas.
'A clerk hadde litherly biset his whyle,
But if he koude a carpenter bigyle.'
And thus they been accorded and ysworn
To wayte a tyme, as I have told biforn.
195   Whan Nicholas had doon thus everideel
And thakked hire aboute the lendes weel,
He kiste hire sweete and taketh his sawtrie,
And pleyeth faste, and maketh melodie.
     Thanne fil it thus, that to the paryssh chirche,
200   Cristes owene werkes for to wirche,
This goode wyf went on an haliday.
Hir forheed shoon as bright as any day,
So was it wasshen whan she leet hir werk.
Now was ther of that chirche a parissh clerk,
205   The which that was ycleped Absolon.
Crul was his heer, and as the gold it shoon,
And strouted as a fanne large and brode;
Ful streight and evene lay his joly shode.
His rode was reed, his eyen greye as goos.
210   With Poules wyndow corven on his shoos,

In hoses rede he wente fetisly.
Yclad he was ful smal and properly
Al in a kirtel of a lyght waget;
Ful faire and thikke been the poyntes set.

215 And therupon he hadde a gay surplys
As whit as is the blosme upon the rys.
A myrie child he was, so God me save.
Wel koude he laten blood, and clippe and shave,
And maken a chartre of lond or acquitaunce.

220 In twenty manere koude he trippe and daunce
After the scole of Oxenforde tho,
And with his legges casten to and fro,
And pleyen songes on a smal rubible;
Therto he song som tyme a loud quynyble;

225 And as wel koude he pleye on a giterne.
In al the toun nas brewhous ne taverne
That he ne visited with his solas,
Ther any gaylard tappestere was.
But sooth to seyn, he was somdeel squaymous

230 Of fartyng, and of speche daungerous.
    This Absolon, that jolif was and gay,
Gooth with a sencer on the haliday,
Sensynge the wyves of the parisshe faste;
And many a lovely look on hem he caste,

235 And namely on this carpenteris wyf.
To looke on hire hym thoughte a myrie lyf,
She was so propre and sweete and likerous.
I dar wel seyn, if she hadde been a mous,
And he a cat, he wolde hire hente anon.

240 This parissh clerk, this joly Absolon,
Hath in his herte swich a love-longynge
That of no wyf took he noon offrynge;
For curteisie, he seyde, he wolde noon.
    The moone, whan it was nyght, ful brighte shoon,

245 And Absolon his gyterne hath ytake;
   For paramours he thoghte for to wake.
   And forth he gooth, jolif and amorous,
   Til he cam to the carpenteres hous
   A litel after cokkes hadde ycrowe,
250 And dressed hym up by a shot-wyndowe
   That was upon the carpenteris wal.
   He syngeth in his voys gentil and smal,
   'Now, deere lady, if thy wille be,
   I praye yow that ye wole rewe on me,'
255 Ful wel acordaunt to his gyternynge.
   This carpenter awook, and herde him synge,
   And spak unto his wyf, and seyde anon,
   'What! Alison! Herestow nat Absolon,
   That chaunteth thus under oure boures wal?'
260 And she answerde hir housbonde therwithal,
   'Yis, God woot, John, I heere it every deel.'
    This passeth forth; what wol ye bet than weel?
   Fro day to day this joly Absolon
   So woweth hire that hym is wo bigon.
265 He waketh al the nyght and al the day;
   He kembeth his lokkes brode, and made hym gay;
   He woweth hire by meenes and brocage,
   And swoor he wolde been hir owene page;
   He syngeth, brokkynge as a nyghtyngale;
270 He sente hire pyment, meeth, and spiced ale,
   And wafres, pipyng hoot out of the gleede;
   And, for she was of town, he profred meede;
   For som folk wol ben wonnen for richesse,
   And somme for strokes, and somme for gentillesse.
275 Somtyme, to shewe his lightnesse and maistrye,
   He pleyeth Herodes upon a scaffold hye.
   But what availleth hym as in this cas?
   She loveth so this hende Nicholas

That Absolon may blowe the bukkes horn;
280 He ne hadde for his labour but a scorn.
And thus she maketh Absolon hire ape,
And al his ernest turneth til a jape.
Ful sooth is this proverbe, it is no lye,
Men seyn right thus: 'Alwey the nye slye
285 Meketh the ferre leeve to be looth.'
For though that Absolon be wood or wrooth,
By cause that he fer was from hire sight,
This nye Nicholas stood in his light.
    Now ber thee wel, thou hende Nicholas,
290 For Absolon may waille and synge 'allas.'
And so bifel it on a Saterday,
This carpenter was goon til Osenay;
And hende Nicholas and Alisoun
Acorded been to this conclusioun,
295 That Nicholas shal shapen hym a wyle
This sely jalous housbonde to bigyle;
And if so be the game wente aright,
She sholde slepen in his arm al nyght,
For this was his desir and hire also.
300 And right anon, withouten wordes mo,
This Nicholas no lenger wolde tarie,
But dooth ful softe unto his chambre carie
Bothe mete and drynke for a day or tweye,
And to hire housbonde bad hire for to seye,
305 If that he axed after Nicholas,
She sholde seye she nyste where he was;
Of al that day she saugh hym nat with ye;
She trowed that he was in maladye,
For, for no cry hir mayde koude hym calle,
310 He nolde answere for thyng that myghte falle.
    This passeth forth al thilke Saterday,
That Nicholas stille in his chambre lay,

And eet and sleep, or dide what hym leste,
Til Sonday, that the sonne gooth to reste.
315 This sely carpenter hath greet merveyle
Of Nicholas, or what thyng myghte hym eyle,
And seyde, 'I am adrad, by Seint Thomas,
It stondeth nat aright with Nicholas.
God shilde that he deyde sodeynly!
320 This world is now ful tikel, sikerly.
I saugh today a cors yborn to chirche
That now, on Monday last, I saugh hym wirche.
    'Go up,' quod he unto his knave anoon,
'Clepe at his dore, or knokke with a stoon.
325 Looke how it is, and tel me boldely.'
    This knave gooth hym up ful sturdily,
And at the chambre dore whil that he stood,
He cride and knokked as that he were wood,
'What, how! What do ye, maister Nicholay?
330 How may ye slepen al the longe day?'
    But al for noght; he herde nat a word.
An hole he foond, ful lowe upon a bord,
Ther as the cat was wont in for to crepe,
And at that hole he looked in ful depe,
335 And at the laste he hadde of hym a sight.
This Nicholas sat evere capyng upright,
As he had kiked on the newe moone.
Adoun he gooth, and tolde his maister soone
In what array he saugh this ilke man.
340 This carpenter to blessen hym bigan,
And seyde, 'Help us, Seinte Frydeswyde!
A man woot litel what hym shal bityde.
This man is falle, with his astromye,
In some woodnesse or in som agonye.
345 I thoghte ay wel how that it sholde be!
Men sholde nat knowe of Goddes pryvetee.

Ye, blessed be alwey a lewed man
That noght but oonly his bileve kan!
So ferde another clerk with astromye;
350 He walked in the feeldes for to prye
Upon the sterres, what ther sholde bifalle,
Til he was in a marle-pit yfalle;
He saugh nat that. But yet, by Seint Thomas,
Me reweth soore of hende Nicholas.
355 He shal be rated of his studiyng,
If that I may, by Jhesus, hevene kyng!
Get me a staf, that I may underspore,
Whil that thou, Robyn, hevest up the dore.
He shal out of his studiyng, as I gesse.'
360 And to the chambre dore he gan hym dresse.
His knave was a strong carl for the nones,
And by the haspe he haaf it of atones;
Into the floor the dore fil anon.
This Nicholas sat ay as stille as stoon,
365 And evere caped upward into the eir.
This carpenter wende he were in despeir,
And hente hym by the sholdres myghtily,
And shook hym harde, and cride spitously,
'What! Nicholay! What, how! What, looke adoun!
370 Awak, and thenk on Cristes passioun!
I crouche thee from elves and fro wightes.'
Therwith the nyght-spel seyde he anon-rightes
On foure halves of the hous aboute,
And on the thresshfold of the dore withoute:
375 'Jhesu Crist and Seinte Benedight,
Blesse this hous from every wikked wight,
For nyghtes verye, the white *pater-noster!*
Where wentestow, Seinte Petres soster?'
And atte laste this hende Nicholas
380 Gan for to sik soore, and seyde, 'Allas!

Shal al the world be lost eftsoones now?'
    This carpenter answerde, 'What seystow?
What! Thynk on God, as we doon, men that swynke.'
    This Nicholas answerde, 'Fecche me drynke,
385 And after wol I speke in pryvetee
Of certeyn thyng that toucheth me and thee.
I wol telle it noon oother man, certeyn.'
    This carpenter goth doun, and comth ageyn,
And broghte of myghty ale a large quart;
390 And whan that ech of hem had dronke his part,
This Nicholas his dore faste shette,
And doun the carpenter by hym he sette.
    He seyde 'John, myn hooste, lief and deere,
Thou shalt upon thy trouthe swere me heere
395 That to no wight thou shalt this conseil wreye,
For it is Cristes conseil that I seye,
And if thou telle it man, thou art forlore;
For this vengeaunce thou shalt han therfore,
That if thou wreye me, thou shalt be wood.'
400 'Nay, Crist forbede it, for his hooly blood!'
Quod tho this sely man, 'I nam no labbe,
Ne, though I seye, I nam nat lief to gabbe.
Sey what thou wolt, I shal it nevere telle
To child ne wyf, by hym that harwed helle!'
405   'Now John,' quod Nicholas, 'I wol nat lye;
I have yfounde in myn astrologye,
As I have looked in the moone bright,
That now a Monday next, at quarter nyght,
Shal falle a reyn, and that so wilde and wood
410 That half so greet was nevere Noes flood.
This world,' he seyde, 'in lasse than an hour
Shal al be dreynt, so hidous is the shour.
Thus shal mankynde drenche, and lese hir lyf.'
    This carpenter answerde, 'Allas, my wyf!

415 And shal she drenche? Allas, myn Alisoun!'
For sorwe of this he fil almoost adoun,
And seyde, 'Is ther no remedie in this cas?'
    'Why, yis, for Gode,' quod hende Nicholas,
'If thou wolt werken after loore and reed.
420 Thou mayst nat werken after thyn owene heed;
For thus seith Salomon, that was ful trewe:
"Werk al by conseil, and thou shalt nat rewe."
And if thou werken wolt by good conseil,
I undertake, withouten mast and seyl,
425 Yet shal I saven hire and thee and me.
Hastow nat herd hou saved was Noe,
Whan that oure Lord hadde warned hym biforn
That al the world with water sholde be lorn?'
    'Yis,' quod this Carpenter, 'ful yoore ago.'
430   'Hastou nat herd,' quod Nicholas, 'also
The sorwe of Noe with his felaweshipe,
Er that he myghte gete his wyf to shipe?
Hym hadde be levere, I dar wel undertake,
At thilke tyme, than alle his wetheres blake
435 That she hadde had a ship hirself allone.
And therfore, woostou what is best to doone?
This asketh haste, and of an hastif thyng
Men may nat preche or maken tariyng.
    'Anon go gete us faste into this in
440 A knedyng trogh, or ellis a kymelyn,
For ech of us, but looke that they be large,
In which we mowe swymme as in a barge,
And han therinne vitaille suffisant
But for a day – fy on the remenant!
445 The water shal aslake and goon away
Aboute pryme upon the nexte day.
But Robyn may nat wite of this, thy knave,
Ne eek thy mayde Gille I may nat save;

Axe nat why, for though thou aske me,
450   I wol nat tellen Goddes pryvetee.
Suffiseth thee, but if thy wittes madde,
To han as greet a grace as Noe hadde.
Thy wyf shal I wel saven, out of doute.
Go now thy wey, and speed thee heer-aboute.
455   'But whan thou hast, for hire and thee and me,
Ygeten us thise knedyng tubbes thre,
Thanne shaltow hange hem in the roof ful hye,
That no man of oure purveiaunce espye.
And whan thou thus hast doon as I have seyd,
460   And hast oure vitaille faire in hem yleyd,
And eek an ax to smyte the corde atwo,
Whan that the water comth, that we may go
And breke an hole an heigh, upon the gable,
Unto the gardyn-ward, over the stable,
465   That we may frely passen forth oure way,
Whan that the grete shour is goon away.
Thanne shaltou swymme as myrie, I undertake,
As dooth the white doke after hire drake.
Thanne wol I clepe, "How, Alison! How, John!
470   Be myrie, for the flood wol passe anon."
And thou wolt seyn, "Hayl, maister Nicholay!
Good morwe, I se thee wel, for it is day."
And thanne shul we be lordes al oure lyf
Of al the world, as Noe and his wyf.
475   'But of o thyng I warne thee ful right:
Be wel avysed on that ilke nyght
That we ben entred into shippes bord,
That noon of us ne speke nat a word,
Ne clepe, ne crie, but be in his preyere;
480   For it is Goddes owene heeste deere.
'Thy wyf and thou moote hange fer atwynne;
For that bitwixe yow shal be no synne,

Namoore in lookyng than ther shal in deede.
This ordinance is seyd. Go, God thee speede!
485 Tomorwe at nyght, whan men ben alle aslepe,
Into oure knedyng-tubbes wol we crepe,
And sitten there, abidyng Goddes grace.
Go now thy wey; I have no lenger space
To make of this no lenger sermonyng.
490 Men seyn thus, "sende the wise, and sey no thyng."
Thou art so wys, it needeth thee nat teche.
Go, save oure lyf, and that I the biseche.'
This sely carpenter goth forth his wey.
Ful ofte he seide 'Allas and weylawey,'
495 And to his wyf he tolde his pryvetee,
And she was war, and knew it bet than he,
What al this queynte cast was for to seye.
But nathelees she ferde as she wolde deye,
And seyde, 'Allas! go forth thy wey anon,
500 Help us to scape, or we been dede echon!
I am thy trewe, verray wedded wyf;
Go, deere spouse, and help to save oure lyf.'
Lo, which a greet thyng is affeccioun!
Men may dyen of ymaginacioun,
505 So depe may impressioun be take.
This sely carpenter bigynneth quake;
Hym thynketh verraily that he may see
Noees flood come walwynge as the see
To drenchen Alisoun, his hony deere.
510 He wepeth, weyleth, maketh sory cheere;
He siketh with ful many a sory swogh;
He gooth and geteth hym a knedyng trogh,
And after that a tubbe and a kymelyn,
And pryvely he sente hem to his in,
515 And heng hem in the roof in pryvetee.
His owene hand he made laddres thre,

25

To clymben by the ronges and the stalkes
Unto the tubbes hangynge in the balkes,
And hem vitailled, bothe trogh and tubbe,
520 With breed, and chese, and good ale in a jubbe,
Suffisynge right ynogh as for a day.
But er that he hadde maad al this array,
He sente his knave, and eek his wenche also,
Upon his nede to London for to go.
525 And on the Monday, whan it drow to nyght,
He shette his dore withoute candel-lyght,
And dressed alle thyng as it sholde be.
And shortly, up they clomben alle thre;
They seten stille wel a furlong way.
530 'Now, *Pater-noster*, clom!' seyde Nicholay,
And 'Clom!' quod John, and 'Clom!' seyde Alisoun.
This carpenter seyde his devocioun,
And stille he sit, and biddeth his preyere,
Awaitynge on the reyn, if he it heere.
535 The dede sleep, for wery bisynesse,
Fil on this carpenter right, as I gesse,
Aboute corfew-tyme, or litel moore;
For travaille of his goost he groneth soore,
And eft he routeth, for his heed myslay.
540 Doun of the laddre stalketh Nicholay,
And Alisoun ful softe adoun she spedde;
Withouten wordes mo they goon to bedde,
Ther as the carpenter is wont to lye.
Ther was the revel and the melodye;
545 And thus lith Alison and Nicholas,
In bisynesse of myrthe and of solas,
Til that the belle of laudes gan to rynge,
And freres in the chauncel gonne synge.
This parissh clerk, this amorous Absolon,
550 That is for love alwey so wo bigon,

Upon the Monday was at Oseneye
With compaignye, hym to disporte and pleye,
And axed upon cas a cloisterer
Ful prively after John the carpenter;
555 And he drough hym apart out of the chirche,
And seyde, 'I noot; I saugh hym heere nat wirche
Syn Saterday; I trowe that he be went
For tymber, ther oure abbot hath hym sent;
For he is wont for tymber for to go
560 And dwellen at the grange a day or two;
Or elles he is at his hous, certeyn.
Where that he be, I kan nat soothly seyn.'
    This Absolon ful joly was and light,
And thoghte, 'Now is tyme to wake al nyght,
565 For sikirly I saugh hym nat stirynge
Aboute his dore, syn day bigan to sprynge.
    'So moot I thryve, I shal, at cokkes crowe,
Ful pryvely knokken at his wyndowe
That stant ful lowe upon his boures wal.
570 To Alison now wol I tellen al
My love-longynge, for yet I shal nat mysse
That at the leeste wey I shal hire kisse.
Som maner confort shal I have, parfay.
My mouth hath icched al this longe day;
575 That is a signe of kissyng atte leeste.
Al nyght me mette eek I was at a feeste.
Therfore I wol go slepe an houre or tweye,
And al the nyght thanne wol I wake and pleye.'
    Whan that the firste cok hath crowe, anon
580 Up rist this joly lovere Absolon,
And hym arraieth gay, at poynt-devys.
But first he cheweth greyn and lycorys,
To smellen sweete, er he hadde kembd his heer.
Under his tonge a trewe-love he beer,

585   For therby wende he to ben gracious.
        He rometh to the carpenteres hous,
        And stille he stant under the shot-wyndowe –
        Unto his brest it raughte, it was so lowe –
        And softe he cougheth with a semy soun:
590   'What do ye, hony-comb, sweete Alisoun,
        My faire bryd, my sweete cynamome?
        Awaketh, lemman myn, and speketh to me!
        Wel litel thynken ye upon my wo,
        That for youre love I swete ther I go.
595   No wonder is thogh that I swelte and swete;
        I moorne as dooth a lamb after the tete.
        Ywis, lemman, I have swich love-longynge
        That lik a turtel trewe is my moornynge.
        I may nat ete na moore than a mayde.'
600   'Go fro the wyndow, Jakke fool,' she sayde;
        'As help me God, it wol nat be "com pa me."
        I love another – and elles I were to blame –
        Wel bet than thee, by Jhesu, Absolon.
        Go forth thy wey, or I wol caste a ston,
605   And lat me slepe, a twenty devel wey!'
          'Allas,' quod Absolon, 'and weylawey,
        That trewe love was evere so yvel biset!
        Thanne kysse me, syn it may be no bet,
        For Jhesus love, and for the love of me.'
610   'Wiltow thanne go thy wey therwith?' quod she.
          'Ye, certes, lemman,' quod this Absolon.
        'Thanne make thee redy,' quod she, 'I come anon.'
        And unto Nicholas she seyde stille,
        'Now hust, and thou shalt laughen al thy fille.'
615   This Absolon doun sette hym on his knees
        And seyde, 'I am a lord at alle degrees;
        For after this I hope ther cometh moore.
        Lemman, thy grace, and sweete bryd, thyn oore!'

The wyndow she undoth, and that in haste.
620 'Have do,' quod she, 'com of, and speed the faste,
Lest that oure neighebores thee espie.'
This Absolon gan wype his mouth ful drie.
Derk was the nyght as pich, or as the cole,
And at the wyndow out she putte hir hole,
625 And Absolon, hym fil no bet ne wers,
But with his mouth he kiste hir naked ers
Ful savourly, er he were war of this.
Abak he stirte, and thoughte it was amys,
For wel he wiste a womman hath no berd.
630 He felte a thyng al rough and long yherd,
And seyde, 'Fy! allas! what have I do?'
'Tehee!' quod she, and clapte the wyndow to,
And Absolon gooth forth a sory pas.
'A berd! A berd!' quod hende Nicholas,
635 'By Goddes corpus, this goth faire and weel.'
This sely Absolon herde every deel,
And on his lippe he gan for anger byte,
And to hymself he seyde, 'I shal thee quyte.'
Who rubbeth now, who froteth now his lippes
640 With dust, with sond, with straw, with clooth, with
    chippes,
But Absolon, that seith ful ofte, 'Allas!'
'My soule bitake I unto Sathanas,
But me were levere than al this toun,' quod he,
'Of this despit awroken for to be.
645 Allas,' quod he, 'allas, I ne hadde ybleynt!'
His hoote love was coold and al yqueynt;
For fro that tyme that he hadde kist hir ers,
Of paramours he sette nat a kers,
For he was heeled of his maladie.
650 Ful ofte paramours he gan deffie,
And weep as dooth a child that is ybete.

A softe paas he wente over the strete
Until a smyth men cleped daun Gerveys,
That in his forge smythed plough harneys;
655 He sharpeth shaar and kultour bisily.
This Absolon knokketh al esily,
And seyde, 'Undo, Gerveys, and that anon.'
'What, who artow?' 'It am I, Absolon.'
'What, Absolon! for Cristes sweete tree,
660 Why rise ye so rathe? Ey, benedicitee!
What eyleth yow? Som gay gerl, God it woot,
Hath broght yow thus upon the viritoot.
By Seinte Note, ye woot wel what I mene.'
This Absolon ne roghte nat a bene
665 Of al his pley; no word agayn he yaf;
He hadde moore tow on his distaf
Than Gerveys knew, and seyde, 'Freend so deere,
That hoote kultour in the chymenee heere,
As lene it me; I have therwith to doone,
670 And I wol brynge it thee agayn ful soone.'
Gerveys answerde, 'Certes, were it gold,
Or in a poke nobles alle untold,
Thou sholdest have, as I am trewe smyth.
Ey, Cristes foo! What wol ye do therwith?'
675 'Therof,' quod Absolon, 'be as be may.
I shal wel telle it thee to-morwe day' –
And caughte the kultour by the colde stele.
Ful softe out at the dore he gan to stele,
And wente unto the carpenteris wal.
680 He cogheth first, and knokketh therwithal
Upon the wyndowe, right as he dide er.
This Alison answerde, 'Who is ther
That knokketh so? I warante it a theef.'
'Why, nay,' quod he, 'God woot, my sweete leef,
685 I am thyn Absolon, my deerelyng.

Of gold,' quod he, 'I have thee broght a ryng.
My mooder yaf it me, so God me save;
Ful fyn it is, and therto wel ygrave.
This wol I yeve thee, if thou me kisse.'

690   This Nicholas was risen for to pisse,
And thoughte he wolde amenden al the jape;
He sholde kisse his ers er that he scape.
And up the wyndowe dide he hastily,
And out his ers he putteth pryvely

695   Over the buttok, to the haunche-bon;
And therwith spak this clerk, this Absolon,
'Spek, sweete bryd, I noot nat where thou art.'
    This Nicholas anon leet fle a fart
As greet as it had been a thonder-dent,

700   That with the strook he was almoost yblent;
And he was redy with his iren hoot,
And Nicholas amydde the ers he smoot.
    Of gooth the skyn an hande-brede aboute,
The hoote kultour brende so his toute,

705   And for the smert he wende for to dye.
As he were wood, for wo he gan to crye,
'Help! Water! Water! Help, for Goddes herte!'
    This carpenter out of his slomber sterte,
And herde oon crien 'water!' as he were wood,

710   And thoughte, 'Allas, now comth Nowelis flood!'
He sit hym up withouten wordes mo,
And with his ax he smoot the corde atwo,
And doun gooth al; he foond neither to selle,
Ne breed ne ale, til he cam to the celle

715   Upon the floor, and ther aswowne he lay.
    Up stirte hire Alison and Nicholay,
And criden 'Out' and 'Harrow' in the strete.
The neighebores, bothe smale and grete,
In ronnen for to gauren on this man,

720 That yet aswowne lay, bothe pale and wan,
For with the fal he brosten hadde his arm.
But stonde he moste unto his owene harm;
For whan he spak, he was anon bore doun
With hende Nicholas and Alisoun.

725 They tolden every man that he was wood;
He was agast so of Nowelis flood
Thurgh fantasie that of his vanytee
He hadde yboght hym knedyng tubbes thre,
And hadde hem hanged in the roof above;

730 And that he preyed hem, for Goddes love,
To sitten in the roof, *par compaignye*.
  The folk gan laughen at his fantasye;
Into the roof they kiken and they cape,
And turned al his harm unto a jape.

735 For what so that this carpenter answerde,
It was for noght; no man his reson herde.
With othes grete he was so sworn adoun
That he was holde wood in al the toun;
For every clerk anonright heeld with oother.

740 They seyde, 'The man is wood, my leeve brother';
And every wight gan laughen at this stryf.
Thus swyved was this carpenteris wyf,
For al his kepyng and his jalousye,
And Absolon hath kist hir nether ye,

745 And Nicholas is scalded in the towte.
This tale is doon, and God save al the rowte!

Heere endeth the Millere his tale.

The Reeve's Prologue

The prologe of the Reves Tale.

Whan folk hadde laughen at this nyce cas
Of Absolon and hende Nicholas,
Diverse folk diversely they seyde,
750 But for the moore part they loughe and pleyde.
Ne at this tale I saugh no man hym greve,
But it were oonly Osewold the Reve.
By cause he was of carpenteris craft,
A litel ire is in his herte ylaft;
755 He gan to grucche, and blamed it a lite.
    'So theek,' quod he, 'ful wel koude I thee quite
With bleryng of a proud milleres ye,
If that me liste speke of ribaudye.
But ik am oold; me list not pley for age;
760 Gras tyme is doon; my fodder is now forage;
This white top writeth myne olde yeris,
Myn herte is also mowled as myne heris,
But if I fare as dooth an open-ers –
That ilke fruyt is ever lenger the wers,
765 Til it be roten in mullok or in stree.
We olde men, I drede, so fare we:
Til we be roten, kan we nat be rype;
We hoppen alwey whil that the world wol pype.
For in oure wyl ther stiketh evere a nayl,
770 To have an hoor heed and a grene tayl,
As hath a leek; for thogh oure myght be goon,
Oure wyl desireth folie evere in oon.
For whan we may nat doon, than wol we speke;
Yet in oure asshen olde is fyr yreke.
775   'Foure gleedes han we, which I shal devyse –

33

Avauntyng, liyng, anger, coveitise;
Thise foure sparkles longen unto eelde.
Oure olde lemes mowe wel been unweelde,
But wyl ne shal nat faillen, that is sooth.
780 And yet ik have alwey a coltes tooth,
As many a yeer as it is passed henne
Syn that my tappe of lif bigan to renne.
For sikerly, whan I was bore, anon
Deeth drough the tappe of lyf and leet it gon,
785 And ever sithe hath so the tappe yronne
Til that almoost al empty is the tonne.
The streem of lyf now droppeth on the chymbe.
The sely tonge may wel rynge and chymbe
Of wrecchednesse that passed is ful yoore;
790 With olde folk, save dotage, is namoore!'
    Whan that oure Hoost hadde herd this sermonyng,
He gan to speke as lordly as a kyng.
He seide, 'What amounteth al this wit?
What shul we speke alday of hooly writ?
795 The devel made a reve for to preche,
Or of a soutere a shipman or a leche.
Sey forth thy tale, and tarie nat the tyme.
Lo Depeford, and it is half-wey pryme!
Lo Grenewych, ther many a shrewe is inne!
800 It were al tyme thy tale to bigynne.'
    'Now, sires,' quod this Osewold the Reve,
'I pray yow alle that ye nat yow greve,
Thogh I answere, and somdeel sette his howve;
For leveful is with force force of-showve.
805   'This dronke Millere hath ytoold us heer
How that bigyled was a carpenteer,
Peraventure in scorn, for I am oon.
And, by youre leve, I shal hym quite anoon;

Right in his cherles termes wol I speke.
810   I pray to God his nekke mote to-breke;
    He kan wel in myn eye seen a stalke,
    But in his owene he kan nat seen a balke.'

Notes

The Miller's Tale is the second of Chaucer's *Canterbury Tales*, a collection of stories told by different tellers. Chaucer organized his collection as a competition between a group of people of different occupations who had met at the Tabard inn in Southwark before setting out on the pilgrimage to Canterbury. A pilgrimage was a journey to a saint's shrine, usually undertaken to benefit the pilgrim's soul, but some people went on pilgrimages for social reasons, or for the pleasure of travel. Chaucer's pilgrims decide to increase the pleasure of their journey by holding a story-telling competition. Whoever tells tales which give best instruction (*sentence*) and most enjoyment (*solas*) will win a free meal at a grand supper to be paid for by the other pilgrims. This scheme has wonderful psychological plausibility but it also results in an interesting set of contrasts. The pilgrims are competing with each other in telling stories, but they are collaborating in making the journey more enjoyable. Some are driven primarily by religious purposes, while others have secular pleasures in view. Some try to win the competition with the morality of their teaching, while others like the Miller aim to amuse the company.

The Canterbury Tales comprises three types of material: the tales, representing the different types of medieval story (such as romances, animal fables, moral stories and saints' lives); the *General Prologue*, which describes the pilgrims and outlines Chaucer's plan; and the link passages (such as *The Miller's Prologue*), in which the pilgrims react to the tale they have just heard and prepare for the next. Chaucer's plan for *The Canterbury Tales* was left incomplete at his death, so we do not know how he would have worked out all the tensions among his pilgrims. *The Miller's Tale* is less affected by this than some others, since we can see how the Miller's personality and his reaction to *The Knight's Tale* influence his tale, and how it in turn stung the Reeve into telling his.

One of Chaucer's main techniques throughout *The Canterbury Tales* is irony. A simple definition would say that irony involves saying one thing while meaning something very different. In line 15, for example, Chaucer speaks of the Miller's 'courtesy', but since he is speaking of the Miller's refusal to defer to people, the opposite meaning 'rudeness' is implied. Much of the humour of *The Miller's Tale* results from a contradiction between words and actions or between an expression and its intended meaning. For example, courtly language may accompany an extremely vulgar action (see lines 168–73). In such a case the language (and the ideal of the class which uses it) is mocked. Sometimes a word is used mainly to mean one thing but another, more critical meaning is present in the background. In line 453 Nicholas undertakes to 'save' Alison from the flood, but his whole purpose in inventing the prophecy is to commit adultery with her, so the opposite meaning of damning her is also implied.

The Miller's portrait:
General Prologue

In the *General Prologue* Chaucer gives descriptions of all the pilgrims. Usually these mix observations about their occupations with character descriptions and moral comment. The Miller is described overwhelmingly in physical terms. He is strong and ugly, loud and foul-mouthed, and he cheats his customers. Can you find anything redeeming in this portrait? The tales Chaucer gives his pilgrims fit their descriptions in the *General Prologue* in different ways. Sometimes there is a close similarity, sometimes the tale reveals a facet of the pilgrim we could not have guessed at, and sometimes the attribution of a tale to a particular teller appears quite arbitrary. How well does *The Miller's Tale* fit in with his portrait? (See p. 9.)

545 **stout carl**   strong rogue (*carl* has overtones of vice, like other words for the lower classes, such as churl or villein).
    for the nones   indeed.
546 **brawn**   muscle.
547 **over al ther he cam**   wherever he went.
548 The ram would be the prize in the wrestling competition.
549 It is hard to reconcile *short-sholdred* with *brood* (broad) and *thikke* (sturdy). Perhaps his forearms or his neck were short while his shoulders were broad. *Knarre* usually means 'crag', so perhaps 'rugged man'.
550 **nolde heve of harre**   would not lift off its hinges.
551 **rennyng**   running.
    heed   head.
552 **berd**   beard.
    reed   red. What is the effect of these comparisons with animals?
552–7 The medieval science of physiognomy aimed to determine people's character on the basis of their faces. In the medieval manuals red hair and large nostrils (*nosethirles* [line 557]) were said to indicate anger, foolishness and lechery. A large mouth suggested gluttony and boldness. See W.C. Curry, *Chaucer and the Medieval Sciences* for further details.
553 **therto**   in addition.
554 **cop**   top.
555 **werte**   wart.
    toft of herys   tuft of hairs.
556 **erys**   ears.
558 **bokeler**   small shield.
    bar   carried, wore.
559 **forneys**   oven, or perhaps cauldron.
560 **janglere**   chatterer, teller of tales.
    goliardeys   buffoon, joker.
561 **harlotries**   indecency. *That* refers to his jokes and tales.
562 **tollen thries**   take three times the accepted payment.
563 Millers judged grain with their thumbs, so a golden thumb might imply that he made large profits, but there is also an allusion to the proverb: *an honest miller hath a golden thumb* which implies that there are no honest millers.
565 **sowne**   play, sound.

The Miller's Prologue

Reactions to *The Knight's Tale*: lines 1–11

When they have heard *The Knight's Tale*, all the pilgrims, both young and old, but especially those of noble birth, agree that it is a noble story and worthy to be remembered. Pleased with this opening tale, the Host, Harry Baily, proposes that another impressive pilgrim, the Monk, who acts more like a nobleman than a priest, should tell the next. Why do you think he does this? (See pp. 103–6)

1   **Whan**   when.
     ytoold   told. In Middle English the past participle often has a *y-* prefix.
2   **route** company.
2–3   **nas ther... seyde**   there was none of them either young or old who did not (*ne*) say (in Modern English, they all said it was).
3   **noble storie**   The Knight told a philosophical romance, a story of two young princes who fell in love with the princess they saw from their prison window, and fought for her. Through the help (and the cruelty) of the pagan gods, Arcite won the battle but was immediately crushed by his horse, leaving his rival Palamon to marry Emily many years later. The story has a noble subject (idealistic courtly love), noble characters, and is told in a way which illustrates the Knight's understanding of the highest conventions of story-telling. The pilgrims may have considered it noble for all (or any) of these reasons. Some of them may not have reacted favourably to its 'superiority'. The basic plot situation of *The Knight's Tale* has some similarities with *The Miller's Tale* in that both concern a girl with two lovers, both involve some sort of supernatural intervention and both raise questions about the justice of fate.
4   **drawen to memorie**   impress on their memories. Medieval psychology proposed that the mind had three segments, or faculties, one of which was memory.

5 **namely**   especially.

gentils   those of noble birth. Who would these pilgrims be?

everichon   everyone, all of them. Is Chaucer implying that the Knight's romance was addressed more to the nobles than to the commoners?

6 **Hooste**   host. Harry Baily, the innkeeper (or host) at the Tabard, has agreed to accompany the pilgrims on their journey and to preside over the story-telling competition.

lough   laughed.

So moot I gon   As I may prosper (a common medieval oath).

7 **aright**   well.

unbokeled   unbuckled, opened.

male   bag. The Host means only that the story-telling has begun, but there may be further implications. Once a bag or a box has been opened it may be hard to close it again. Unexpected or uncontrollable things may emerge.

8 **Lat se**   let us see.

10 Monks were people who swore to remove themselves from the world and devote themselves to prayer and contemplation. In the *General Prologue* the Monk is described as a jolly and manly man, a noble prelate who is preoccupied with hunting and good food. Roast swan is his favourite dish. In the medieval social hierarchy it would have seemed fitting to go from a representative of the secular ruling class (the Knight) to a high-ranking churchman.

konne   know how to.

11 **quite with**   reply to, but also perhaps 'repay' or 'rival'.

The Miller's interruption: lines 12–35

The Miller, who is already drunk and in no condition to remember his manners, interrupts the Host, declaring in a loud voice that he will tell the next tale. He brushes aside the Host's attempt to restrain him and announces that his tale will be about a carpenter, his wife, and the student who becomes her lover. What do we learn about the Miller's character? Why does he apologize for his drunkenness (lines 29–32) when he has only just put himself forward so forcefully (lines 16–19, 24–5)? What can we learn about the Host from his three very different speeches in *The Miller's Prologue* (lines 6–11, 21–3, 26–7)?

12 **for dronken** because of being drunk.

13 **unnethe** hardly.

14 **nolde** (= *ne wolde*) would not.
    avalen take off. The doffing of hats, and the uncovering of the head when speaking to a superior, were expected forms of politeness (compare with line 15).

15 **abyde** defer to. The mention of *his curteisie* may be ironic, in that the Miller's brand of courtesy is not courtesy at all.

16 **Pilates voys** a loud, ranting voice (suitable for playing the role of Pontius Pilate in the Mystery Plays). The Mystery Plays were a sequence of short plays telling significant episodes of Christian history, from the creation to the last judgement. They were performed in the open air in many English towns on Corpus Christi day (one of the great festivals of the Christian calendar, which usually occurs in June) between about 1375 and 1576. The main focus of the cycle of plays was the life of Jesus Christ, and within that Pilate, the Roman governor of Palestine who condemned Christ to death, was an important villain. The nature of the role and the conditions of performance require a loud ranting voice. It is interesting that although the plays only began to be performed in his lifetime, Chaucer can already use the actors' ranting as a proverbial expression of loudness. There are several references to the Mystery Plays in *The Miller's Tale*. They may represent a conscious attempt by Chaucer to relate this tale to popular culture.
    gan to crie cried out (past tense).

17 The Miller swears by the arms, blood and bones of Christ, a blasphemous but colourful oath.

18 **kan** know.
    for the nones for the occasion. The Miller is using the word 'noble' in an aggressively ironic sense.

19 Is the Miller merely repeating the Host's word (*quite* [line 11]) or is he giving it a more forceful twist? Could it be somewhat aggressive to use the same word while intending a stronger meaning?

21 **Abyd** wait.
   leeve dear.

22 **bettre** higher on the social scale. But perhaps, in view of line 27, the Host also privately means 'morally better'. Medieval people usually thought of the social world as very strictly organized in order of rank. The pilgrimage is one of the few occasions on which people from different classes could mix on terms of rough equality. Even on the pilgrimage the Host tries to retain some aspects of the social order. Do you think the Host means to be rude to the Miller here?

23 **werken thriftily** act properly, arrange things fittingly. Perhaps the Miller does not accept the Host's idea of the proper way to behave.

25 **elles** else.
   go my wey travel on my own. The Miller's threat to leave the company reminds us that the Host's authority to regulate the pilgrimage (which the pilgrims agreed to in the *General Prologue*) rests on the consent of the other pilgrims.

26 **a devel wey** in the devil's name.

27 **wit** reason. The Host means that drink has made the Miller irrational (in the *General Prologue* he is often compared to animals), but the Host is the one who *is overcome* in the argument.

28 **herkneth** listen.
   alle and some one and all, everyone.

29 **protestacioun** solemn declaration. The word has implications of a legal plea, or of a statement denying blame. The Miller may be using it humorously.

30 From the sound of my voice I know that I am drunk.

31 **mysspeke or seye** speak or say anything wrong (the prefix *mys-* applies to both verbs).

32 **Wyte it** blame it on. The Tabard inn, from which the pilgrims set out earlier in the morning was in Southwark (*Southwerk*). Perhaps we should be amused that it is the Host's own beer (which he was happy to sell) that is now disrupting his plans.

33 **legende and a lyf** story and a biography. In many contexts the phrase would suggest that the speaker intends to tell the life of a saint (a common type of story to medieval audiences).

35 **clerk** student.

set the wrightes cappe   deceived the carpenter. Because of the
mention of the carpenter's wife in the previous line, everyone
would assume (rightly) that the deception involved is adultery.
Do you think this story sounds like a saint's life?

The Reeve's objection: lines 36–58

The Reeve urges the Miller not to speak, since he assumes that a
story about a deceived carpenter will inevitably be an attack on
him, because he used to be a carpenter. But the Miller pushes his
objection aside, explaining that only married men can be
cuckolds, that there are many virtuous women, and that the best
way to avoid becoming a cuckold is not to enquire too closely
into your wife's secrets. This raises two problems: the medieval
(and renaissance) attitude to adultery and the implications of the
Miller's rather oblique reply.

Although the Church always condemned all types of
adultery (which the seventh commandment forbids [Exodus 20:
14]), social attitudes to sex outside marriage were rather
different. Hardly any blame was attached to young men who
seduced married women (seducing a virgin was regarded as an
offence). While women were blamed if they had lovers (and
could sometimes suffer very severe penalties) it was almost
expected that given the chance they would. This reflects both the
fact that most marriages were arranged (with the result that
romantic love would often only exist outside marriage) and the
offensively low view which most men took of women's moral
standards. The husband of the woman who took a lover was
termed a cuckold (*cokewold* [line 44]), a figure of fun, treated with
derision by his contemporaries. It seems as though it was the
honour of the husband (and perhaps of the wife's brothers) that
was at stake in cases of adultery. In this male-dominated society
the anxiety which the men felt about the sexual fidelity of their
wives was transferred into an endless series of jokes, so that
(surprisingly to us) any mention of cuckolds was likely to be

greeted with howls of laughter from both sexes (though for different reasons). In many medieval stories (and especially in *fabliaux* – see Notes pp. 49–50) it was expected that an old man marrying a younger woman would be made a cuckold. Nor was it any use for the husband to try to evade his fate, for the jealous husband was an equally ridiculous figure (at least in literature).

The Reeve appears to think that the honour of himself, his wife and women generally is at risk in the tale the Miller is about to tell. The Miller's reply is rather evasive. He makes three statements: first, you cannot be a cuckold if you have no wife (line 44); second, there are many good women for every bad one (line 47); and third, that it is best not to enquire too carefully into your wife's secrets (lines 50–8). While the second appears to be reassuring, the third creates further anxiety. The first is ambiguous and the Miller pointedly refers it to the marital situation of the Reeve.

36 **Reve**   reeve, estate-manager.
   Stynt thy clappe   stop your chatter.
37 **Lat be**   let go, stop.
   lewed   ignorant (or perhaps, lascivious).
   harlotrye   crude stories, ribald talk.
38 **eek**   also.
39 **apeyren**   injure.
   hym defame   defame him, spoil his reputation.
40 **swich**   such.
   fame   disrepute.
41 You may say as much as you like about other matters. Although the Reeve here says that defamation in general and slandering women are sinful, his own tale does both.
42 **spak ful soone ageyn**   replied immediately.
43 What is the tone of 'dear brother' here?
44 **cokewold**   cuckold, betrayed husband (see Notes above). This phrase may be a proverb. It states that only a husband can be a cuckold. It may also imply that all husbands are cuckolds.
45 **oon**   one. What is the effect of *therefore* (for that reason)?
46 **ful**   very.

47 And always a thousand good ones for every bad one. The
   Miller's expression looks like borrowed wisdom. Chaucer uses
   almost the same phrase in the Prologue to *The Legend of Good
   Women* (G text, line 277). It also appears in *The Mirror of
   Marriage* by the French poet Eustache Deschamps (?1340–1406).

48 **knowestow** (= *thou knowest*) you know.
   but if thou madde unless you are mad.

49 **artow** (= *art thou*) are you.
   tale words, talk.

50 **pardee** certainly. Although this oath originally meant 'by
   God', its force had become weakened by familiarity.
   as wel as thow as much as you, just as you have.

51 **nolde** (= *ne wolde*) would not want. The Miller regards the
   oxen in his plough team as valuable possessions which he
   would not want to lose. Some critics think there may be a link
   between the horns of the oxen and the (proverbial) horns of
   the cuckold.

52–3 Take upon myself the extra burden (literally, more than
   enough) of believing that I am one (that is, a cuckold).

54 **wol bileve wel** shall firmly believe.
   noon not one, none.

55 **nat** not.
   inquisityf inquisitive, curious.

56 About God's secrets (*pryvetee*) or those of a wife. Medieval
   Christians believed that it was not up to human beings to
   question God's reasons. But *pryvetee* can also mean 'private
   parts', and the next line makes it clear that the Miller intends
   the pun, warning married men that as long as they have
   satisfaction from their wives, they should not enquire too much
   about their wives' other sexual activities.

57 **So** as long as, provided that.
   foyson plenty. There is a very striking (not to say shocking)
   contrast here between the theological phrase 'God's plenty' and
   what it refers to (sexual activity).

58 There is no need (*nedeth nat*) to enquire about the rest
   (*remenant*).

Chaucer's apology: lines 59–78

Chaucer ends *The Miller's Prologue* by speaking in his own voice, as the narrator of the whole *Canterbury Tales*. He warns his readers that the Miller and the Reeve are scoundrels who are going to tell dirty stories, and advises those who want a more improving tale to read a different one. Do you think that Chaucer is really trying to spare the embarrassment of his more pious readers? Is it, as Alfred David says in his book *The Strumpet Muse*, 'an obvious come-on' designed to attract readers? Or is Chaucer simply trying to avoid responsibility for what he has written? It is worth remembering that until recently many readers did 'turn the page' (line 69), regarding *The Miller's Tale* as unfit for proper discussion or serious study.

60 He would not restrain (*forbere*) his words out of respect for anyone.

61 **cherles**   churl's, rascal's. Churl was a descriptive term for the lowest class in medieval society. The word was also used to describe immoral or impolite behaviour. Some of these meanings survive in the Modern English word 'churlish'. In general Chaucer uses this common word rather infrequently, so the two occurrences (lines 61, 74) here might imply strong condemnation. On the other hand Chaucer might be questioning the applicability of the word, asking what it means if we dismiss the Miller and the Reeve as churls.

    manere   manner, own way.

62 **M'athynketh**   it displeases me, I regret.

    reherce   relate, repeat.

63 **gentil**   noble, well-born. Just as terms describing the lower class were used to convey negative sentiments, so *gentil* came to signify positive qualities, such as compassion, sensitivity and goodness. *Gentillesse* (line 71), a key medieval term whose implications are debated in *The Canterbury Tales*, denoted both the behaviour appropriate to someone of noble birth and virtuous action more generally. *Gentil* could also be used as a polite (or flattering) form of address.

    wight   person.

47

64 **demeth nat that I seye**   do not think that I speak.

65 **Of yvel entente**   with an evil intention.

66 **Hir**   their.

   bettre   better (probably he means morally better).

67 **falsen**   falsify.

   mateere   subject-matter. As in the *General Prologue* (lines 725–42), Chaucer explains that he has no wish to write down the crude story which follows, but his obligation to tell the truth about the pilgrimage compels him to.

68 **whoso list it nat yheere**   whoever does not wish to hear it. This line implies an audience of listeners, the next line an audience of readers. Both types of audience were possible at the time. The poet might declaim his poem before the court, but manuscript copies were made which others could read to themselves, or to an audience of their family and friends.

69 **leef**   page.

   chese   choose.

70 **ynowe**   enough.

71 Historical (*storial*) matter concerning noble behaviour (*gentillesse*, see Note to line 63 above). Chaucer would probably have regarded some of the moral legends (such as *The Sergeant of the Law's Tale* and *The Second Nun's Tale*) as historical.

73 **amys**   wrongly.

75 **mo**   more.

76 **harlotrie**   crude stories.

77 **Avyseth yow**   Consider this.

78 **maken ernest of game**   take as serious (*ernest*) what is playful (*game*). *Ernest* and *game* (joke) are proverbial opposites in Middle English, but Chaucer often makes jokes about things he means seriously. What guidance is Chaucer giving us about how to read *The Miller's Tale*? Can we trust it?

The Miller's Tale

The Miller's Tale belongs to the genre of the *fabliau* (plural *fabliaux*). *Fabliaux* are defined as 'short funny stories in the vernacular' (that is in the local language of everyday speech, rather than in Latin, the universal learned language). They usually involve an act of deception and a misdeed, usually connected with sex or excretion. The *fabliaux* contain a fairly restricted cast of characters: a cunning woman (who may trick either her husband or a prospective lover), a prostitute, a jealous old husband, a lecherous student, a merchant or a priest. The characters are usually not developed as individuals, but are defined by their gender and their social position. Usually one of the group (in most cases the husband) is victimized and humiliated by some of the others. Scholars have been able to identify three types of *fabliau* (crudely, the second flood, the misdirected kiss, and the branding) which Chaucer combined in order to produce the plot of *The Miller's Tale*. Most of the *fabliaux* which survive are written in Old French, and were composed in northern France between about 1190 and 1340. There are also several German *fabliaux* from the thirteenth century, and a few in Dutch. (It is in fact possible that the Dutch/Flemish *fabliaux* are earlier than the French ones.) There is considerable debate about the audience of the *fabliaux*. Some writers see them as an anarchic and popular form of literature, while others think they were an aristocratic form (a way of looking down on the peasants), pointing out that they are often found in expensive manuscripts, and that if noble characters appear they are never the victims. Students often appear in the *fabliaux* and usually get the better of other characters. That Chaucer, who wrote most of the *fabliaux* in Middle English, always gives them to lower class tellers may indicate that he regarded the form as popular. (For further discussion of the *fabliau* see pp. 106–9 and the examples in the Appendix, pp. 196–8).

For the moment it is important to mention that while Chaucer adapted the form (for example, by introducing far more characterization and a considerable amount of parody) he also abided by most of its basic assumptions (many of which we would regard as sexist). In a *fabliau* it was expected that students would be lecherous, that young wives would take lovers, and that old husbands would be jealous and become cuckolds. We must be alert for the variations which Chaucer plays on these themes, rather than expecting him to do without them.

Introduction and portrait of Nicholas: lines 79–112

The tale opens, in an apparently leisurely way, with descriptions of the main characters. These descriptions abound in details of fourteenth-century life, but they also convey a good deal of information and expectation on which the plot will later depend. Nicholas is a student, but his main interest is in astrology. He is an expert in 'secret love' and a fine musician. We learn about his character from a tour of his room, which contains herbs, stones, textbooks, scientific equipment, and a musical instrument, the psaltery. Do these tell us more about his studies or his hobbies? In fact the description of Nicholas is rather like the thumbnail sketches of the pilgrims in the *General Prologue*. It might be interesting to compare it with those of the Miller (see p. 9) and the Clerk (see p. 193). What conclusions should we draw from Nicholas's combination of foresight, secrecy, love and music? (See pp. 118–23.)

79 **Whilom** Once. *Whilom ther was* is almost as traditional an opening formula as the Modern English 'Once upon a time'.
Oxenford Oxford. J.A.W. Bennett shows that the main background details from *The Miller's Tale* can be paralleled (and brought to life) from Oxford's historical records (*Chaucer at Oxford and Cambridge*, pp. 26–57). Although this does not

prove that Chaucer knew Oxford well, it demonstrates the realism of the tale.

80 **gnof** churl, lout. This is the only occurrence of the word in Middle English literature, which may mean that it was a colloquial term of abuse. (It also implies that this meaning, which scholars agree on, must be regarded as a guess only.) The carpenter is rich enough to have a servant and a maid as well as a large house, but he still does manual work.

gestes heeld to bord took in lodgers.

81 **craft** trade.

82 **poure scoler** poor scholar. This may represent a formula often found in legal documents, or it may (in view of Nicholas's expensive possessions) be ironic.

83 **art** the arts course. In medieval universities, all students studied the arts course (which in theory consisted of all seven liberal arts [grammar, logic, rhetoric, arithmetic, geometry, music and astronomy], but in practice concentrated mainly on logic) before going on to one of the higher faculties (law, medicine and theology). Since the description mentions no higher faculty but emphasizes astrology, presumably Nicholas is still studying the arts course. But the word 'art' can be applied to astrology (see line 101), so Chaucer may be using the same word to denote his official and his actual studies.

fantasye imagination, desire.

84 **turned** directed. In the Middle Ages astrology (*astrologye*) was not completely distinguished from astronomy. The position of the stars at someone's birth was widely believed to influence character, and the movements of the planets were thought to cause changes in emotions and even the onset of diseases. In some respects this is similar to modern interest in horoscopes, but it also went further in that a good deal of medical practice depended on the position of the stars (see the description of the Doctor of Physic in the *General Prologue*). Although many of these practices were tolerated, the Church was opposed to attempts to foretell the future on the basis of the stars, which is what Nicholas is interested in. In his *Treatise on the Astrolabe*, Chaucer states his disbelief in astrological prediction (*Riverside Chaucer*, p. 671), but in his poems he often introduces changes of weather (see line 88) with

reference to the position of the stars. Like other Christian poets exploiting myths about the pagan Gods, he may have regarded this as a matter more of poetic practice than of belief.

85 And understood (*koude*) some (*a certeyn*) of the propositions (*conclusiouns*). The implication is that Nicholas's knowledge of the art is limited. He knows (or thinks he knows) how to predict some things but not others.

86 **demen** judge, decide.
   interrogaciouns questions.

87 **certein houres** the exact time.

88 **droghte or elles shoures** dry weather or rain. Apparently the carpenter believes in Nicholas's ability to predict the weather (see lines 406–14).

89 **bifalle** happen.

90 **rekene** count.
   hem them.

91 The word *clerk* has a range of uses. Any learned man, or anyone who was studying beyond the elementary level could be called a *clerk*. But the word could also be used more strictly of the priesthood (clergy). When Absolon is called a *parissh clerk* though, he is neither a student nor a priest but an assistant to the priest. (See line 204.)
   cleped called.
   hende courteous. This word is used eleven times in the tale. *The Oxford English Dictionary* lists a range of meanings: 'near, at hand; handy, ready or skilful with the hand; pleasant in dealing with others; courteous, gracious; nice'. Critics have suggested that Chaucer plays with all these meanings at different points in the tale.

92 **deerne** secret.
   solas pleasure, delight (perhaps with sexual implications here).

93 **sleigh** sly, cunning.
   privee discreet, secretive. We should also remember the puns on *pryvetee* (line 56).

94 **meke** gentle, submissive, innocent. Here the emphasis is on appearance (*to see*). *Mayden* can mean a virgin of either sex. (See p. 145.)

95 **chambre** bedroom. *Hostelrye* usually means inn or pub, but

can also be used of student lodgings or a large house (compare with *in* [line 439]).

96   Nicholas has a room to himself. This is required by the plot, but it may also be an indication of his wealth, since medieval students usually shared rooms. This line repeats a line from *The Knight's Tale*, which describes Arcite's tragic feeling of loneliness as death approaches:

> **What is this world? What asketh men to have?**
> **Now with his love, now in his colde grave**
> **Allone, withouten any compaignye.**   **(2777–79)**

The Miller's use of this line may be deliberate parody, or the repetition might be accidental. The phrase also appears in Chaucer's *Tale of Melibee* (line 1560).

97   Very handsomely decorated with sweet-smelling herbs.

99   **lycorys**   liquorice.
     cetewale   setwall, zedoary (a spice resembling ginger).

100   **Almageste**   astronomy textbook. *Almagest* is the common medieval title for the great astronomy textbook of the Greek scientist Claudius Ptolomaeus (Ptolemy), who was active between 127 and 148 AD. This title derives from an Arabic adaptation of the work's Greek nickname *megistee* (meaning 'the greatest'). This is a neat illustration of the way that Greek scientific knowledge was preserved and cultivated by Islamic scientists before being passed back via Islamic Spain to medieval western Europe. In the later Middle Ages *Almagest* became a generic term for the astronomy textbook, so Nicholas owned an astronomy textbook, which may or may not have been Ptolemy's book. Ptolemy also wrote a famous textbook of astrology, the *Tetrabiblos*. Books (all of which had to be copied by hand) were extremely expensive in the Middle Ages, so Nicholas's library of large and small books indicates wealth.

101   An astrolabe (*astrelabie*) is a scientific instrument, a set of flat circular metal plates, with two pointers, which can be used to measure the position of the planets. For his son Lewis, Chaucer wrote *A Treatise on the Astrolabe*, which describes the construction and use of the instrument. Although astrolabes

are not rare, relatively few students would have owned one.

longynge for   belonging to.

102 **augrym stones**   counting stones. These were stones or
counters with Arabic numerals on them, which could be placed
on a marked board and used as a type of abacus.

faire apart   neatly on their own.

103 **couched**   placed.

104 **presse**   cupboard.

faldyng   coarse woollen cloth.

105 **al above**   on top of everything.

gay   elegant. A psaltery (*sautrie*) was a stringed instrument like
a small harp. The Clerk in the *General Prologue*, who is rather
different from Nicholas, would rather have philosophy books
than an elegant psaltery (line 296). What does this tell us about
Nicholas's priorities?

108 *Angelus ad virginem* (Latin, meaning 'The angel to the virgin') is
the first line, and therefore the title, of a well-known song about
the Annunciation, the episode in the Bible in which the angel
Gabriel visits the Virgin Mary to tell her that she has been
chosen to give birth to God's son Jesus. (Modern recordings of
this song have been released, including one by the Tallis
Scholars.) Do you think we should take this as evidence of
Nicholas's religious devotion, or is there an irony in view of his
behaviour later in the tale? (See p. 141.)

song   sung.

109 **the Kynges Noote**   the King's tune (probably a popular song
of the time, but not so far firmly identified).

110 **myrie**   tuneful. Do you think this line means that he sang a
lot, or that those who heard him often blessed him for his
songs?

111 Why is he a *sweete clerk*?

112 **After**   according to.

freendes fyndyng   the gifts of his friends.

rente   income. Do you think there might be some criticism
here? The portrait of the Clerk in the *General Prologue* (lines
299–302, see p. 193) also refers to the friends who subsidize his
studies.

The carpenter's marriage: lines 113–24

The carpenter is used as a point of departure for both portraits. Nicholas is his lodger, and Alison is his wife. The marriage is recent; the wife young and 'wild' (*wylde* [line 117]), the husband old and jealous (*Jalous* [line 116]). The Miller allows himself a few conventional comments (and a not very learned quotation) on the problems of marriage. Perhaps the passage encourages us to think of John and Alison at first as 'types', a view which will be modified as the tale proceeds.

113 **newe** recently. Strictly *wyf* means 'woman' (as opposed to maiden), but here (and throughout this tale) 'wife' seems the most appropriate modern equivalent.

116 **heeld hire narwe in cage** kept her closely confined. It appears that the *cage* here is metaphorical; there are French *fabliaux* in which it is literal.

117 Why is she called *wylde*? Do you think that this is the Miller's prejudice and that really she is just young (*yong*), or is she already being likened to an animal?

118 Do you think *been lik* means 'likely to become' or just 'like'?

119 Cato (*Catoun*) here refers to the book of short proverbs which was used in medieval schools as the most elementary Latin reader. If you had not read 'Cato', you had not read anything. No doubt the book derived some of its prestige from a supposed link with the Roman Cato the elder (234–149 BC), famous for the pithy expression of traditional moral values.
rude uneducated, ignorant.

120 **bad** advised.
his simylitude someone like him.

121 **after hire estaat** according to their position (here, in age; usually, in society).

122 **elde** old age.
at debaat at odds, quarrelling. This expression is proverbial. It also expresses a continuing theme of *The Canterbury Tales*.

123 **sith** since. Why does the Miller call marriage a *snare*? Should we link this with the *cage* (line 116)?

124 **care** trouble. Does this expression denote sympathy or is it generalized and empty? Is the Miller philosophical or smug?

Portrait of the carpenter's wife: lines 125–62

The detailed description of the heroine was an important set-piece in the romance, and a subject for courtly love lyrics. In this description Chaucer seems to be parodying such poetic portraits, comparing the carpenter's wife (from now on I shall call her Alison, but we do not actually learn her name until line 258) with the domestic and everyday, where the court poets would have chosen exotic and valuable objects of comparison. (See pp. 123–6.)

Should we see the portrait as an amusing parody, as an image of wholesome sexuality, or as a shameless fantasy of a woman's body presented for the amusement of a male audience? Charles Muscatine (*Chaucer and the French Tradition*, p. 229) points out that although Chaucer adapts and parodies the conventions of courtly descriptions, he still follows the same set of categories:

the fairness, the eye, the bent brows, the hue, the voice, the mouth, the carriage, the silken costume, the jewelry, the accomplishments.

125 **Fair** beautiful.
therwithal besides, also.

126 **wezele** weasel.
gent delicate.
smal slender. What are the implications of this unusual comparison?

127 She wore (*werede*) a belt (*ceynt*) decorated with strips (*barred*)

entirely (*al*) of silk. Just possibly *al* could qualify *barred*, and mean 'all over'.

128 **barmclooth**   apron.
whit   white.
morne   morning.

129 **lendes**   loins.
goore   fold, flounce.

130 **smok**   shift, slip (worn under the apron, and visible above it).

130–1 **broyden... coler**   embroidered all over the front (*bifoore*) and back (*bihynde*) and around the collar (*coler*). The punctuation here is by the modern editor. If it were removed, the clothes would have to be understood differently (for example, one might take the collar as black, rather than the embroidery).

132 With black silk, both inside and outside. If the collar is open, then embroidery on the inside could be seen. Should we think of the expense of all the embroidery on this white *smok* (line 130) or of the attention it attracts? What is the effect of the pervasive and strong contrast of black and white?

133 **tapes**   ribbons (which hold her cap [*voluper*] in place).

134 **suyte**   pattern.

135 **filet brood**   wide headband. It is placed very high to show off her forehead.

136 **sikerly**   certainly.
likerous ye   lustful eye.

137 **Ful smale ypulled**   very finely plucked.

138 **tho**   those.
bent   curved, arched.
blake   black.
sloo   sloe-berry.

139 **blisful**   delightful.
on to see   to look on.

140 **pere-jonette**   early ripening pear.

141 Is there any reason for thinking that the wool (*wolle*) of the male sheep (*wether*) is especially soft? How soft is Alison and in what way?

142 **girdel**   belt.
heeng   hung.

143 **perled... latoun**   decorated with brass beads.

144 **to seken... doun**   wherever you might look.

145 **nys** (= *ne is*) is not (but the whole phrase means 'is no man', see A Note on Chaucer's English, p. 177).

thenche   think, imagine. It would be an ordinary compliment to say: 'nowhere in the world is there any woman like her'; but after setting up this expectation, the Miller first frustrates it (no *man*), and then produces an even more extreme statement (nowhere in the world is there anyone so wise [*wys*] as to be able to imagine her). This is an example of witty hyperbole, which is also self-deflating, since Alison is an imaginary construction of Chaucer's.

146 Such a joyful pet or such a wench. After such a build up neither expression is exactly complimentary. *Popelote* (poppet) suggests a doll, beautiful and undemanding, while *wenche* implies coarseness and sexual availability. (See p. 123.)

147 **hewe**   colouring, complexion.

148 **Tour**   Tower of London, where coins, including the noble (worth a third of a pound sterling) were minted (*yforged*). This expression seems to draw together (partly through wordplay) some of the themes of the description so far: cages, newness, brightness, money, and social status (noble/wench). It continues the tendency to compare her with valuable (and exchangeable?) objects.

149 **yerne**   lively. Alison's voice is stronger than a courtly lady's would be.

150 **swalwe**   swallow.

  berne   barn.

151 **Therto**   in addition, moreover.

  make game   gambol, be playful.

152 **dame**   mother.

153 **bragot**   bragget (an alcoholic drink made by fermenting ale and honey).

  meeth   mead (fermented honey and water). What is the effect of talking about Alison's taste and comparing her with sweet intoxicating drinks? Perhaps there is poetry in the physicality of these comparisons.

154 **hoord**   store.

  heeth   heather. But we do not know that people stored apples in heather.

155 **Wynsynge**   skittish, lively.
   joly   high-spirited, frisky.
156 As tall as a mast and as straight as a bolt (of a crossbow).
157–8 On her low-cut collar she wore a brooch which was as wide as
   the boss of a shield (*bokeler*). Or perhaps the collar is low
   because it is open (see Note to line 132, p. 57). Why would
   Alison wear a large brooch here?
160 Both *prymerole* (primrose) and *piggesnye* (pig's eye) are flowers.
   They emphasize Alison's passive beauty and again associate her
   with the natural world. Or we could think of both words as
   affectionate names.
161 **leggen**   lay.
162 In a spirit of realism, the Miller suggests different ways in
   which she could trade on her beauty: by marrying an honest
   free-born man (*good yeman*), probably a little above her in the
   social scale; or by briefly becoming the mistress of someone
   much more important, a lord. Does this imply criticism or
   admiration of the different choice (marrying a fairly rich old
   tradesman) she has in fact made?

Nicholas molests Alison: lines 163–98

After describing two of his four main characters, the Miller sets
his plot in motion. Nicholas takes advantage of the carpenter's
absence to declare his love for Alison, and to grab hold of her
thighs. With a short protest, and a little persuasion, she grants
him her love, and they agree to trick the carpenter.

The comedy of this passage depends on a contrast between
Nicholas's very rude actions and his use of the elaborate and
polite language of courtly romance. In courtly romances and
love-lyrics, the lover tended to present himself as the inferior of
his lady, as her worshipper and her servant. He spoke of the pain
he felt, almost amounting to death, and (in religious terms) of
his need of her mercy. Conventionally the lover made a secret of
his affection, so as not to compromise his lady's honour.

Although such lovers always pretended an entirely selfless devotion, content to admire the lady and to receive the occasional kind glance in return, in practice most of them aimed at a sexual relationship. This means that Nicholas's inappropriate use of the language of courtly romance (lines 169–80) is an exposé of the truth (in that the courtier-lovers pretend to be pure but are really like Nicholas) as well as a witty parody. Audiences accustomed to *fabliaux* would probably have been amused rather than outraged by Nicholas's behaviour in this context. You may disagree.

163 **eft** again.
    so bifel the cas it so happened.
164 **on a day** one day. On *hende* (courteous) see Note to line 91, p. 52.
165 **Fil** began.
    rage sport (with a sexual sense, as there is also in *pleye* here).
166 **Oseneye** Osney, now a part of Oxford, but then a village outside, with a large abbey, where the carpenter often worked, as we learn later on (lines 553–60).
167 **ful queynte** very sly. Why *As* (since)?
168 **prively** secretly. There is no doubt about where Nicholas grabs her. *Queynte* means 'elegant, pleasing thing' and is used as a euphemism for vagina. There may be a pun on the similar sounding 'cunt', as vulgar in Middle English as it is today.
169–70 **Ywis... spille** Indeed, unless I obtain what I desire, my love (*lemman*), I shall die (*spille*) for secret love of you. *Lemman*, *derne* and *spille* are common words in courtly love poetry, but there the lover would not make his threat (the same one) so promptly, or with Nicholas's accompanying action. Some critics regard *spille* as an obscene pun, since it can also mean 'ejaculate'.
171 **haunchebones** thighs.
172 **al atones** at once, immediately.
173 **also... save** God preserve me.
174 **sproong** leaped, sprang.
    trave frame in which unruly horses were restrained while they

were shod. How is this image appropriate to Alison and her situation?

175 **wryed** twisted. Alison twisted her head (*heed*) rapidly away from Nicholas to make it more difficult for him to kiss her.

176 **by my fey** on my honour. Notice that Alison here uses the familiar form (*thee* – see A Note on Chaucer's English, p. 176). This form can express intimacy, a sense of superiority (a person would say 'thee' to inferiors, but 'you' to superiors), or scorn. Which do you think Alison intends here? You may find it interesting to pay attention to the way she switches between familiar and polite forms.

177 **lat be** stop, give over.
quod said.

178 *Harrow, out* and *allas* are all cries of distress. Notice that Alison threatens to cry out, rather than simply doing so.

179 Take your hands off, for goodness sake.

180 In his role of courtly lover Nicholas begged (*gan... crye*) for pity from his lady. But there is a satirical contrast between the language and the situation here, where Nicholas is molesting Alison, and she asks him to stop.

181 And spoke so graciously (*faire*) and offered his love so insistently (*faste*).

183 Perhaps we should regard Alison's oath (*ooth*) as a reminder of the purpose of the pilgrimage.

184 **comandement** command, disposal.

185 **leyser** opportunity.

186 What evidence do we have of the carpenter's jealousy (*jalousie*)?

187 That unless (*but*) you watch (*wayte*) carefully and are secretive (*privee*).

188 **woot** know.
I nam but deed I am as good as dead (literally, I am nothing but dead).

190 **therof care thee noght** do not worry about that.

191–2 A student would have wasted his time (literally, spent his time badly [*litherly*]) if he did not know how to deceive a carpenter. (See p. 122.)

193 **accorded** agreed.

194 **wayte** watch for, await. The implication of their agreement is that they will wait for a better opportunity.

195 **everideel**   all, every part.
196 **thakked**   patted.
    lendes   loins.
    weel   well.
197 **sawtrie**   psaltery (see Note to line 105, p. 54).
198 **faste**   rapidly, or perhaps intensely. Some critics have
    suggested that music in this tale serves as a codeword for sexual
    activity (compare lines 106 and 544). But any such
    interpretation of this line must take account of the implication
    of line 194.

Portrait of Absolon: lines 199–230

Just when we thought *The Miller's Tale* was a simple story of
adultery, Chaucer introduces his complicating factor, a second
admirer for Alison. There is a large social gulf between the two
lovers. Nicholas has income (line 112) and leisure to pursue his
hobbies (lines 84, 92, 105), whereas Absolon has to work for his
living (line 204). His accomplishments are less intellectual and
more practical: shaving, basic surgery, legal drafting and dancing
(lines 218–22). What do you make of the contrast between their
musical skills (lines 105–10, 223–8)? Should we regard Absolon's
accomplishments as comic, or should we respect him as a 'self-
made man'? (See pp. 126–31.)

Where Absolon's accomplishments reflect the real world of
fourteenth-century Oxford parish clerks, his name is very
uncommon, and may well refer to the biblical Absalom (2
Samuel 13–18). In the Bible Absalom is notable for fair but
treacherous speech, and for his beauty, especially his luxuriant
hair (2 Samuel 14:25–6). His hair caused his downfall because it
caught in a tree allowing his pursuers to catch up with him. The
description of Absolon in the tale is unusual (for a description
of a man) in the amount of physical detail it provides (lines 206–
16). As with the portrait of Alison it may be helpful to think of
it as a parody of the description of a courtly lady which one

would expect to find in a romance (see Appendix, pp. 194–5). There is discussion of his squeamishness and possible effeminacy on pp. 129–31.

200 To perform Christ's own works. That is, to worship God in the way Christ ordered. What is the effect of the contrast with the previous paragraph?

201 **haliday** holy day. 'Holiday' derives from this, since on holy days (Sundays and religious festivals) most people did not work.

202 **shoon** shone.

203 **leet** left, stopped. As today, the homeworker's holiday only begins when the domestic chores are finished. Notice how narrative serves characterization here. Alison goes to the church only in order that we can meet Absolon. Nothing happens until the portrait has been completed.

204 The *parissh clerk* was an assistant to the priest, who helped in various ways in the church services.

206 **Crul** curly.
    heer hair.

207 **strouted as a fanne** spread out like a fan.

208 **evene** smooth.
    shode parting (of his hair). The word *joly* (here, pretty) is often applied to Absolon. Some critics find that the word has associations with sexuality.

209 **reed** red. Both the word *rode* (complexion) and eyes (*eyen*) as grey as a goose are usually found in descriptions of heroines. (Compare Appendix p. 194, line 546.)

210 **Poules wyndow** the window of St Paul's Cathedral. Absolon's shoes have an elaborate design cut out (*corven*) on them (perhaps in the form of a second layer of leather). Presumably the design is a lattice or a circle, like a rose window. The window in question would have belonged to the old cathedral, destroyed by fire in 1666.

211 **hoses rede** red stockings.
    fetisly elegantly. We also find this word in descriptions of courtly ladies.

212 He was dressed (*Yclad*) very delicately (*smal*) and neatly (*proprely*).

213 **kirtel**   tunic.

   waget   sky-blue.

214 It had many beautiful laces (literally the laces [*poyntes*] were placed thickly [*thikke*] and very beautifully [*faire*]).

215 **therupon**   on top of it (the tunic).

   gay surplys   bright (or fine) robe. Nowadays, the surplice is a loose outer robe which only priests wear.

216 **blosme upon the rys**   blossom on the bough. This simile recalls the description of Alison.

217 **so God me save**   as God may preserve me (a common and very weak oath). *Child* (lad) has connotations of forcefulness, vigour. Is this ironic or is Absolon a simpleton?

218 He knew well how to let blood, trim hair and shave. As well as being a parish clerk (only a part-time occupation), Absolon fulfils the duties of a barber. In the Middle Ages bloodletting was a common medical procedure. Medieval doctors usually restricted themselves to the theoretical aspects of medicine (diagnosis and formulating a cure); the practical surgery was left to a barber working to the doctor's instructions. Absolon has mastered an important practical skill, which also indicates the intellectual and social distance between him and Nicholas.

219 And draw documents of land tenure or the release of property (*acquitaunce*). Another example of a practical skill separate from the theoretical law teaching of the university. It might be significant that Absolon has practical skills corresponding to all three higher faculties of the university (see Note to line 83, p. 51).

220 **twenty**   a large number (rather than exactly twenty).

221 **scole**   style. But school can also mean university. Perhaps there is a joke in the apparent seriousness with which the Miller distinguishes styles of dancing. Or perhaps Chaucer is making a joke about the preoccupations of the students.

   tho   at that time, then.

222 **casten**   leap, fling.

223 **rubible**   rebec, a small two-stringed fiddle.

224 **Therto**   to it (that is, with the rebec accompanying).

   quynyble   high treble. Either Absolon is singing falsetto or his voice has not yet broken.

225 **giterne**   gittern, a small plucked four- or five-stringed instrument, the forerunner of the renaissance guitar.

226 **nas**   (= *ne was*) was not. This negative cancels out with *ne*
      (nor). Absolon visited all the pubs with lively barmaids.
      brewhous   pub. Most medieval pubs brewed their own beer.
227 **solas**   entertainment.
228 **gaylard tappestere**   lively barmaid.
229 **sooth**   truth.
      somdeel squaymous   somewhat squeamish.
230 **of speche daungerous**   fastidious of speech (or perhaps,
      sparing of speech). Absolon likes to sing in pubs with lively
      barmaids, but he does not care for all the gross behaviour he
      comes across in them. Notice how the lines speed up to
      describe his music and dancing, whereas the concluding
      reservation holds them back.

Absolon begins to woo Alison: lines 231–61

While he is swinging the censer filled with incense around the
church, Absolon has the chance to admire the women of the
parish. He is so strongly attracted to Alison that he takes his
gittern out to serenade her early the next morning, waking her
and her husband. The exaggeratedly courteous behaviour of the
lover makes a comic contrast with the religious duties he exploits
(and neglects), and the realities of fourteenth-century town life. It
may be courtesy on Absolon's part not to accept any payment,
but what he is actually refusing is the offering which will provide
bread for the poor. It may be amorous to stay up all night and
sing lovesongs, but it will not do any good if (as he must) he
wakes up his mistress's husband.

231 **jolif**   lively, sprightly.
232 **sencer**   censer (the vessel containing the burning incense, like
      a kettle on the end of a chain).
233 Vigorously (*faste*) spreading incense over the women of the
      parish. There were religious festivals which only the women
      would have attended, or perhaps Absolon directs himself
      particularly to their (segregated) part of the church.

234 **lovely** loving.

236 To stare at her seemed to him a happy pastime.

237 **propre** beautiful.
   likerous delightful, attractive (or perhaps flirtatious).

239 **hire hente anon** pounce on her at once. Perhaps this violent simile reveals Absolon's true attitude to Alison.

241 **love-longynge** passionate desire (an expression often found in medieval lovesongs).

242–3 That he would not accept an offering from any of the women. Out of courtesy he said that he did not want any. Courtesy is ambiguous here, meaning both 'politeness' and 'sense of himself as a courtly lover'.

244 **ful brighte shoon** shone very brightly.

245 **ytake** taken.

246 Because he intended to stay up all night (*wake*) for the sake of love.

247 *Jolif* here means 'full of desire', rather than 'pretty'. Consider the other meanings of this word (also spelt *joly*), as applied to Absolon (lines 208, 231, 240, 263).

249 **ycrowe** crowed.

250 **dressed hym** placed himself.
   shot-wyndowe hinged window (a window that shuts). Most medieval windows did not open at all, but this story requires one that does (line 619). In fact it is hinged at the top (lines 632, 693). This is an example of the way in which the realistic descriptions of the early part of the tale prepare elements which will be needed for the plot later.

252 **gentil and smal** fine and high-pitched.

253 **if thy wille be** if it is your wish.

254 **rewe** take pity (a typical expression of courtly love-poetry).

255 **acordaunt to** in harmony with.
   gyternynge gittern-playing (see line 225).

256 **awook** awoke.

258 **Herestow nat** Do you not hear? This is the first mention of Alison's name.

259 **chaunteth thus** sings like this.
   oure boures wal wall of our bedroom. Why does John ask this question?

260 **therwithal** at that.

261 **it every deel**   every part of it. This line conveys Alison's lack
   of interest.

Absolon's methods of wooing: lines 262–88

The Miller leaves the scene by the bedroom window unresolved
(it will be repeated and resolved at lines 586–702), moving on to a
general description of Absolon's attempts to court Alison. We
should probably see this as a parody of the behaviour of a noble
lover. Thus while Absolon suffers for love (feeling miserable and
being unable to sleep [lines 264–5]) and approaches his lady
through an intermediary (line 267) as the noble lover would, his
display of accomplishments (lines 269, 276) and the gifts he offers
(lines 270–2) are very different, reflecting the difference in wealth
and opportunities. Notice how the repeating sentence structure
and the sequence of verbs depict the energy and resourcefulness
of Absolon's wooing. But all his efforts are doomed to failure.
Alison loves courteous or close-at-hand Nicholas, and treats
Absolon as a figure of fun. Do we laugh at Absolon with her or
do we have some understanding for his predicament? If Absolon
seems to be following a model of love which is inappropriate to
his social position, what do we make of the Miller's views about
'normal' amatory behaviour (lines 273–4, 284–5)?

262 This continues: what more do you want to know? (literally,
   'what do you want better than good?').
264 Woos (*woweth*) her so much that he becomes miserable (*hym is
   wo bigon*).
265 **waketh**   remains awake. Chaucer treats this as a typical
   symptom of love in the *General Prologue* (lines 10, 98).
266 **kembeth**   combs.
   made hym gay   made himself look handsome (or perhaps
   joyful).
267 **meenes**   intermediaries, middlemen (but the word can also
   mean 'trick' or 'bribe').

brocage   use of an agent. These words convey an idea of underhand trickery, but there may also be an element of parody, since the courtly lover would usually be so overcome by love that he could only approach his lady through a friend. Absolon may be paying his broker, and in any case we should contrast this with Nicholas's more direct (and more successful) approach.

268 Absolon here imitates the courtly lover, who would offer to serve his lady to show her superiority to him, and his willingness to humble himself. Absolon ranks below a page, and Alison is not noble enough to have one.

269 **brokkynge**   warbling, trilling.
as   like.

270 **pyment**   spiced wine. Absolon brings her mead (*meeth*), but the Miller says she tastes like it (line 153).

271 And cakes (*wafres*), whistling hot out of the embers (*gleede*). The cakes would have been baked close to the fire in the oven.

272 **profred**   offered.
meede   reward, money. Is the Miller casting aspersions on the morals of town girls? A medieval country girl might have less use for money.

273 **wonnen for**   won, or seduced, through.

274 **strokes**   blows. Should we take this as the Miller expressing generalized wisdom (in the sense of 'everyone has different tastes') or does this phrase betray his attitude to women?

275 **lightnesse**   agility.
maistrye   skill (but the word can also mean dominance).

276 Herod (*Herodes*) was one of the most famous roles in the Mystery Plays (see Note to line 16, p. 42), celebrated for the ranting and raving it involved (hence Hamlet's complaint about exaggerated acting: *it out-herods Herod, Hamlet*, 3.2.15). Do you think Absolon's voice and manner suit this type of role? Mystery Plays could be acted on a platform (*scaffold*) or on a pageant wagon.

277 **what availleth hym**   what does it profit him, what good does it do him? Notice how this section deflates the mood of the previous lines.

278 **hende**   courteous (see Note to line 91, p. 52).

279 **blowe the bukkes horn**   blow his horn, go whistle (a proverbial expression indicating that his efforts are futile).

280 He got nothing for his trouble (*labour*) but contempt, derision (*scorn*).

281 **ape** fool.

282 And turns all his seriousness (*ernest*) to (*til*) a joke (*jape*). Compare with line 78.

283 Perhaps the emphasis (*Ful sooth*) here leads us to doubt the truth of the proverb.

284 **right thus** just so, exactly like this.
      nye slye near-by crafty one.

285 Makes the farther off (*ferre*) loved one (*leeve*) to be disliked (*looth*).

286 For even if Absolon should be mad (*wood*) or angry (*wrooth*).

287 **By cause** because.
      fer far.

288 **in his light** in his way (preventing him from being noticed). Notice the concentration of proverbs in this passage.

Alison and Nicholas make their plans: lines 289–310

In the carpenter's absence at Osney (again!), the lovers agree on a plan to deceive him. After telling Alison to say that she does not know where he is, Nicholas retires to his room with food and drink for a couple of days. Obviously he does not expect the carpenter to notice his absence for a while! Is this an agreed plan (line 294) or is Nicholas in control (line 295)?

289 **ber thee wel** conduct yourself well.

291 **bifel it** it happened.

294 **Acorded been** have agreed.

295 **shapen hym a wyle** devise a stratagem, trick.

296 **sely** simple, unfortunate. Does this word imply sympathy or contempt?
      bigyle deceive.

297 Does *game* mean scheme or does it tell us about their attitude?
      wente aright worked, went according to plan.

301 **tarie** remain, delay.
302 **dooth... carie** makes someone carry. Even in small matters
     Nicholas prefers that others should do the work.
     ful softe very discreetly.
303 **mete** food.
     tweye two.
304 **bad** told.
305 **axed** asked.
306 **nyste** (= *ne wiste*) did not know.
307 **ye** eye.
308 **trowed** thought, believed.
     maladye sickness.
309 Because (*For*), in spite of (*for*) any cry her maid could make to
     him.
310 **for... falle** (in spite of) whatever might happen. Nicholas
     thinks that Alison needs detailed instructions, but he is
     confident that she will be able to trick John.

John wonders what has happened to Nicholas: lines 311–39

Nicholas's plan begins to work. By Sunday evening John starts
to wonder what has become of Nicholas, and sends his servant
to find out. The servant cannot obtain an answer, but
eventually, through a hole in the wall catches a glimpse of him
staring upwards. He reports back to John. From lines 317–502,
the tale switches predominantly into direct speech. How does
Chaucer characterize John through the sounds and rhythms of
his voice?

311 **passeth forth** carries on.
     thilke that same.
312 **stille** quietly.
313 **hym leste** pleased him.
314 Until sunset on Sunday.
315 **hath greet merveyle** wondered greatly.

316 **Of** about.
eyle ail, be wrong with.
317 **adrad** afraid. Alison also swore by St Thomas (see line 183). These oaths may reflect Chaucer's knowledge of Oxford, since there was a church of St Thomas at Osney, or there may be a link with the Canterbury pilgrimage.
318 **It stondeth nat aright** all is not well.
319 **shilde** forbid.
320 **ful tikel** very unstable. This banal phrase reveals the shallowness of John's thinking.
321 **saugh** saw.
cors yborn body carried. What does John's amazement at this (presumably commonplace) event tell us about him?
322 **wirche** work.
323 **knave** servant.
325 **boldely** immediately.
326 **sturdily** resolutely, boldly.
328 **cride** shouted. (Compare with Nicholas's plan [line 309].)
331 **noght** nothing. Or at least he gave no sign of hearing.
332 He found (*foond*) a hole at the lower end of a plank (*bord*). The interior walls would have been wooden.
333 **Ther as** where.
wont accustomed. Critics have commented on the amount of detail and explanation here.
334 **depe** deeply. Does this mean he looked intently, or he looked in as far as he could see?
335 **hadde... sight** caught a glimpse of him.
336 **evere capyng upright** continually staring upwards.
337 **As he had kiked** as if he had stared. Presumably he stares like a madman, and the Miller alludes to popular beliefs about the cause of lunacy.
338 **Adoun** down.
soone at once.
339 **array** condition.
ilke same.

John responds to his servant's report: lines 340–65

John attempts to come to terms with his sorrow at Nicholas's distress with a battery of proverbs and exemplary tales. Confident of the wisdom of ordinary people, he feels sure that Nicholas has over-reached himself and fallen into madness. But he also decides to take practical steps to bring him out of his trance. John's thoughts mix elements of wild surmise (lines 343–4, 346), self-satisfaction (lines 345, 347–8), half-appropriate anecdote (lines 349–53), concern (line 354) and very physical forms of assistance (lines 355–64). (See pp. 112–17.)

340 **blessen hym**   cross himself.
341 St Frideswide (died around 735 AD) was supposed to have established a nunnery near Oxford. She became the patroness of the city. There was a parish church of St Frideswide which later became Christ Church Cathedral.
342 Little (*litel*) does a man know what will happen to him.
343 **is falle**   has fallen.
    astromye   astronomy. Does *with* imply that Nicholas has suffered 'as a result' of his astrological interests or 'in spite' of them (in that astrology might claim to give him some warning of catastrophe).
344 **woodnesse**   madness.
345 I always thought it would turn out like this.
346 **pryvetee**   secrets (see Note to line 56, p. 46). The intended irony here is that John is incapable of learning the lesson he teaches. Later in the poem he believes a secret about the future which turns out to be his undoing. There may also be an irony against the Miller, who in replying to the Reeve (line 56) used the same expression as the foolish carpenter uses here. (See p. 156.)
347 **lewed**   ignorant. What ironic point is made by John's praise of ignorance?
348 Who knows nothing apart from the Creed (*bileve*). The Creed is

a statement of basic Christian beliefs which everyone was
expected to know by heart.

349–52   This is a well-known story, versions of which can be found in
Plato's *Theaetetus*, in Diogenes Laertius' *Lives of the
Philosophers*, in *Aesop's Fables* and in Italian *novelle*. It may be a
joke against the carpenter that he tells it as if it were personal
experience because he is ignorant of its history.

349   **ferde**   fared.

350–1   **prye... Upon**   observe.

351   **what... bifalle**   to find out from them what was going to
happen.

352–3   Until he fell into a clay-pit (*marle-pit*). He had not foreseen that.
This story is part of the struggle between the clever and the
foolish which Nicholas began (lines 191–2) and which ends only
at the end of *The Miller's Tale*.

354   **Me reweth soore of**   I am very sorry for.

355   **rated of**   scolded for. In Middle English *studying* has its
modern meaning of 'working to acquire learning', which is
appropriate here, but it can also mean 'being in a state of
mental perplexity', which may suit the sense of 'getting him out
of his trance' implied in line 359.

357   **underspore**   lever (the door) upwards from underneath.
Robin, his servant, will raise the door enough for John to insert
the staff which he will use as a lever to lift the door off its
primitive hinges.

359   **gesse**   imagine, suppose. For *studying* see Note to line 355,
above.

360   **he gan hym dresse**   he turned his attention to (or perhaps, he
went to).

361   Compare with the description of the Miller, *General Prologue*,
line 545, p. 9.

362   He heaved (*haaf*) it off by the fastenings (*haspe*) at once. The
general meaning is clear enough but there is some doubt about
the detail. If 'he' is John, then he heaves the door off its hinges
(a possible meaning for *haspe*) and the door-opening goes
according to plan. If 'he' is Robin then he grabs the door by
the latch (which Nicholas has fastened on the inside) and he is
so strong that he can pull the door off its hinges without a
better hold.

John rouses Nicholas from his trance: lines 366–92

Faced with Nicholas staring upwards, John employs both the means at his disposal: physical force (lines 367–8) and popular religion which amounts almost to magic (lines 369–78). Having put John into a state of alarm and wonder, Nicholas takes control of the situation, promising to tell John secret news after he has had a drink. How does John's use of charms (lines 371–8) fit in with his earlier remarks about religious mysteries (line 346)?

366 **wende** thought. The medieval Christian was in danger of despair (*despeir*) either as a result of commerce with devils, or because of meditating on human sinfulness and the impossibility of meeting God's standards. John thinks Nicholas has fallen into despair. He responds by trying (not very competently) to exorcize any devils present (line 371) and by reminding Nicholas of God's forgiveness of sins as a consequence of Christ's suffering on the cross (line 370).

367 **hente** seized.

368 **spitously** loudly, vehemently.

369 John wants Nicholas to look down (*adoun*) to break the spell of whatever he is staring up at. But it would be more usual to tell people in despair to look up, to the cross or to the heavens.

370 **passioun** suffering (particularly applied to Christ's suffering on the cross on Good Friday).

371 I make the sign of the cross (*crouche*) to protect you from evil spirits (*elves*) and from wicked creatures (*wightes*). *Wight* usually means 'creature, person'. Possibly John uses it in an earlier more malevolent sense, or perhaps he misuses the word, thinking it has connotations of evil.

372 At that (*Therwith*) he said the night charm straightaway (*anon-rightes*). The night-charm (lines 375–8) was a popular prayer, used by ordinary people as a protection against witchcraft.

373 **halves** sides. Presumably he makes the house safe by looking in each of the four directions in turn and then towards the threshold (*thresshfold* [line 374]) of the main doorway. Perhaps he recites the rhyme in each direction.

374 **withoute**   outside. This would be the main entrance of the
house.

375 St Benedict (*Benedight*), roughly 480–547, was the founder of
the orders of monks (see Note to line 10, p. 41) in western
Christianity.

377 The phrase *nyghtes verye* has been much argued over by critics and
editors. Walter Skeat in *The Complete Works*, Vol v, p. 106,
suggested that it might represent the oral survival of an Old
English phrase *for nighte werigum* meaning *against the evil spirits of
the night*. E.T. Donaldson in his essay, 'The Miller's Tale', suggested
that the scribes made a mistake, and that Chaucer wrote *nyghtes
nerye*, which Donaldson glosses as *preserve us at night*.

Pater-noster is Latin for 'Our Father', the most famous of all
Christian prayers. The *White Pater-noster* is a rhyme found in
many European languages in several different versions,
equivalent to:

> Matthew, Mark, Luke and John
> Bless the bed that I lie on.
> Four corners to my bed,
> Four angels round my head;
> One to watch and one to pray
> And two to bear my soul away.

(*The Oxford Dictionary of Nursery Rhymes*, ed. Iona and Peter
Opie, pp. 303–05)
Perhaps John regards the text he recites *as* the *White Pater-noster*
(Walter Skeat in *The Complete Works*, Vol v, p. 106 cites a
variant which is almost a nonsense poem and which involves St
Peter's brother), or perhaps his spell refers to the other rhyme
for extra protection. This rhyme seems to lie on the border
between a prayer (which is part of religion) and a magic spell
(which is forbidden). In the Middle Ages, although some
magical practices were certainly regarded as heathen, the border
between magic and religion may have been fuzzy in places.

378 **wentestow**   did you go. Probably St Peter's sister (about whom
nothing is known) is here for the sake of the rhyme.

380 **Gan... soore**   sighed deeply.

381 **eftsoones now**   right now.

382 **seystow** do you say.

383 **swynke** labour, toil. John carries out his initial plan, seeking to combat what he sees as Nicholas's despair with simple piety.

384 **Fecche** fetch. Is Nicholas thirsty, or is there a psychological purpose?

385 **in pryvetee** privately, in confidence. (Compare with line 346 and see pp. 156–7.)

386 **certeyn... toucheth** something that concerns.

387 **certeyn** for sure.

389 Because of the poor quality of drinking water, most English people drank beer to quench their thirst. Everyday beer consumed at all times of day was rather weak, but the *myghty ale* which John brings up himself (indicating the importance of the conversation?) was strong beer for serious drinking. A *quart* is an exact measure, two pints, a quarter of a gallon. Perhaps *large quart* implies a more approximate, generous amount, or it might refer to the large tankard which they share.

391 Nicholas locked (*faste shette*) the door again, but there is no reference to anyone putting it back on its hinges. This might mean that the door was easy to replace, or perhaps Chaucer forgot that the door had just been levered off.

392 And made the carpenter sit (*sette*) down beside him. Or *sette* may mean 'placed'.

Nicholas tells John about the second flood: lines 393–425

Nicholas begins the conversation by swearing John to secrecy with the threat of divine vengeance and madness. John defensively assures him that he is no tell-tale. This opens the way for Nicholas's revelation: as a result of his astrological speculations he has discovered that the world will be destroyed by a flood the following night. This news appals the carpenter, who is particularly troubled about what will happen to Alison. But Nicholas promises him that there is a way for the three of them to be saved. Why does John believe this story?

393 **hooste** landlord.

    lief dear. Is Nicholas presenting himself to John as dependant (lodger), friend (*lief*), or superior (lines 394–9)?

394 **trouthe** troth, pledged word.

395 That you will not betray (*wreye*) this secret (*conseil*) to any man (*wight*).

397 **telle it man** tell it to anyone.

    forlore utterly lost, damned.

398 **vengeaunce** punishment, revenge.

399 **be wood** go mad. Here John is threatened with madness if he betrays the secret. Later he is treated as mad because he believed it.

400 Christ's blood was an object of veneration in the Middle Ages because by shedding it Christ made possible the forgiveness of sins, and because wine was believed to turn into Christ's blood in the mass. So John's oath is a serious one.

401 **labbe** tell-tale, chatterbox.

402 Nor, though I say (*seye*) it myself, do I enjoy talking too much (*gabbe*).

403 **wolt** wish.

404 **child ne wyf** anyone (literally, child nor woman). Christ harrowed (*harwed*) hell when, after his crucifixion, he went down to hell to free the righteous people from Old Testament times. The story appears only in the apocryphal (that is, 'not regarded as an authentic part of the Bible') *Gospel of Nicodemus*, but it was popular in the Middle Ages, perhaps because it shows Christ in a conventionally heroic role, rescuing prisoners from a castle. The story was dramatized in the English Mystery Plays and in *Piers Plowman*.

    Notice how Nicholas's rhythms and sentence structures enable him to take control in this section.

406 **yfounde** found.

408 **a Monday** on Monday. Since they are speaking on Sunday evening the next Monday will be the following day.

405–13 **at quarter nyght** a quarter of the way through the night.

409 **wilde and wood** strong and violent.

410 The story of the flood and Noah's (*Noes*) ark (from Genesis, 6–8) was a popular one in the Middle Ages, the subject of Mystery

Plays and many types of visual depiction. That his flood should be like Noah's obviously appeals to John on religious grounds. But Nicholas's use of the comparison in deceiving him tells us about John's ignorance (in that God promised never again to destroy the world with water, Genesis 9:11–17) and his conceit (in that Noah was saved because he was the only virtuous man in the world).

411 The ludicrous speed with which the flood will cover the world makes John's credulity seem even more comic. In the Bible it rained for forty days.

412 **dreynt** drowned, submerged.
    hidous dreadful.
    shour downpour.

413 **drenche** drown.

417 **cas** situation (*cas* also has overtones of fate and destiny). Notice that John echoes what Nicholas said as he emerged from his trance (lines 380–1).

419 **werken... reed** act according to learning and advice.

420 **heed** mind, thoughts.

421 **trewe** wise.

422 **conseil** advice.
    rewe be sorry. The phrase occurs in the apocryphal book (see Note to line 404, p. 77) Ecclesiasticus 32:24, and in a work of Albertano of Brescia, where it is attributed to Solomon, and from where Chaucer took it. He also cites the phrase in *The Tale of Melibee* and *The Merchant's Tale*. Here Nicholas uses the authority of Solomon (*Salomon*) to browbeat John.

423 **wolt** wish to.

424 **undertake** promise.
    seyl sail.

Nicholas tells John how to avoid the flood: lines 426–54

Nicholas takes advantage of John's rather dim recollection to retell the story of the flood, laying special stress on the difficulty Noah had in persuading his wife to enter the ark. His conclusion is that John must hurry to provide large vessels in which the three of them will be able to float and therefore avoid drowning. They will need food only for one day, since the flood is due to end within a few hours. Nicholas cleverly mixes story-telling with instructions to maintain his control over John. Why does he emphasize Noah's difficulties with his wife? How does he prevent John from trying to save the servants?

426 **Hastow nat** have you not. In this passage Nicholas moves from rhetorical questions to commands.
  hou how.
428 **lorn** lost, destroyed.
429 **ful yoore ago** a very long time ago.
430–5 This part of the story does not appear in the Bible but it formed a comic interlude in the Mystery Plays. Noah's wife is usually portrayed as a worldly, practical person who regards Noah's communing with God as daydreams, but is later forced to recognize the correctness of his actions.
431 **sorwe** sorrow, trouble.
  felaweshipe companions.
432 **Er** before.
433 I dare well say that he would rather.
434 **thilke** that.
435 Nicholas emphasizes the quarrel between Noah and his wife, rather than their subsequent reconciliation. Notice that he suggests that Noah might have preferred separate boats (an idea not found in other accounts).
436 **woostou** do you know.
437 **asketh** requires.
  hastif urgent.
438 **tariying** delay. Presumably preach (*preche*) is used in the sense of speaking at length.
439 **in** house (especially lodging-house).
440 A kneading trough (*trogh*) was used for kneading dough. According to J.A.W. Bennett (*Chaucer at Oxford and Cambridge*, pp. 4–5), a kimlin (*kymelyn*) was a tray or trough used for baking or brewing. Both vessels needed to be large, fairly shallow and watertight.

442 **mowe**   may.
    swymme   float.
    barge   boat, ship. In Middle English a *barge* is a sea-going vessel.
443 **vitaille**   victuals, food and drink.
    suffisant   enough.
444 **fy on the remenant**   never mind the rest.
445 **aslake**   slacken, diminish, go down.
446 **pryme**   about nine o'clock in the morning.
447 **wite**   know.
448 **eek**   moreover. What is Nicholas's real reason for excluding Gill and Robin?
449 **Axe**   ask.
450 **pryvetee**   secrets.
451 Be satisfied unless you are going mad.
452 **greet**   great.
    grace   mercy, forgiveness (especially God's forgiveness of sinners). This line makes explicit the greatness John is aspiring to. He will receive (and think himself worthy of) the same special grace as Noah.
453 **out of doute**   without doubt, without fear. Nicholas speaks of saving Alison, but he intends to sin with her.
454 **speed thee heer-aboute**   get on with this quickly.

More advice from Nicholas and a warning: lines 455–92

Nicholas's directions become more detailed and more absurd. He even describes the conversation they will have once the boats are floating above the drowned streets of Oxford. Is all this detail primarily for the audience's amusement, or does it also play a part in the deception of John? Perhaps such persuasion involves selling someone a dream. In order to ensure their survival Nicholas insists that there must be silence in the three tubs, while they devote themselves to prayer (line 479), and that no sinful thoughts or looks must pass between John and his wife (lines 482–3). Why does Nicholas emphasize the need for purity and religious devotion? What is his real reason for wanting John's tub far from Alison's? How do we react to him instructing John about sexual morality?

456 **Ygeten** got, obtained.
457 The tubs could have been suspended in the attic above the upper bedrooms, but given that John later falls quite a long way into a place where his neighbours can come to see him, it is more likely that the tubs were suspended from the rafters of the hall, the main room in a medieval house, which was often two storeys high with the inside of the roof exposed.
458 **purveiaunce** preparations, foresight.
460 **faire... yleyd** properly stowed away in them.
461 **corde** rope.
     atwo in two, apart.
462 So that we can float free (*go*) when the water comes.
463 **an heigh** high up, above. The *gable* is the part of the wall (here probably filled in with lath and plaster) which forms the vertical side for the sloping roof. They will float out over the stable (line 464) because it is only one storey high.
464 **gardyn-ward** towards the garden.
466 Perhaps there is a contradiction here. The idea seems to be that the roof will protect them while it is raining, but when it stops (*goon away*) they will want to float out. But this implies that the flood will stop short of the second storey (since the water-level will not rise much after the rain stops) which would defeat the purpose of the flood. This may be a deliberate inconsistency alerting us to a weakness in Nicholas's plan (and to John's foolishness in believing him), or a real, if small, slip by Chaucer.
468 Nicholas evokes an image of marital harmony for John to dream of. This may relate back to the Mystery Play story of Noah, in which the wife becomes submissive after she enters the ark. But why does he envisage them as birds (compare with lines 126, 152, 174) and why is John compared to the female?
469 **clepe** call.
473–4 Where before Nicholas tempts John with Noah's holiness, here

he emphasizes his power. When everyone else is dead the three of them will be the rulers of the world.

475 **o** one.

ful right very seriously.

476 **wel avysed** very careful.

477 **shippes bord** on board ship (that is, in their tubs).

479 Why does Nicholas insist that rather than calling out or lamenting, they should be at prayer?

480 **heeste deere** precious command.

481 **moote... atwynne** must hang far apart.

482 The preaching of the Church took such a negative attitude to sexuality that even though (under the right circumstances) sex between married people was not regarded as sinful, John may well have thought that it was. Or perhaps the special circumstances of the second flood make it easier for Nicholas to convince John of the danger of sexual sin. There may also be an allusion to the tradition, believed by many early theologians and reported in medieval sermons, that there was no sexual activity in the ark. It may be worth remembering that on some interpretations the first flood was caused by sexual sin (Genesis 6:1–7).

483 **deede** action. Nicholas's reference to sinful glances and actions has been taken as an allusion to a passage from Jesus's 'Sermon on the Mount', Matthew 5:27–8:

Ye have heard that it was said by them of old, Thou shalt not commit adultery; but I say unto you that whosoever looketh on a woman to lust after her hath committed adultery with her already in his heart.

Do you think this parallel helps Nicholas persuade John?

484 **ordinance is seyd** command has been given.

487 **abidyng... grace** awaiting the fulfilment of God's will.

488 **space** time.

489 *Sermonyng* means both 'preaching' and 'speaking at length'.

490 A proverb. If you send a wise man on an errand, you do not need to give detailed instructions. But he *has* given detailed instructions!

491 **it... teche** it is unnecessary to tell you what to do. Nicholas's

plan should ensure that he and Alison can spend the night together, but what does he intend to do when the flood does not come?

John prepares for the flood: lines 493–524

John tells Alison about the danger from the flood and begins to carry out Nicholas's instructions in order to save them all. The Miller pokes fun at John in several different ways: by calling him foolish (line 493), by telling us what Alison is really thinking (line 496), thus making her words (lines 499–502) ironic, and by an exclamation in his own voice (lines 503–5). Notice the preponderance of verbs as he describes John's frantic activity in carrying out Nicholas's strange orders (lines 506–24).

494 **weylawey** alas.
495 John thinks the secret has become his, but it is no secret from Alison (line 496). She knows his private thoughts because Nicholas has told her what they will be. This transfer of secrets from the lovers to the husband parallels the transfer of Alison's *pryvetee* (see line 56) from John to Nicholas.
496 **war** aware.
    bet better.
497 **queynte cast** elaborate trick.
    seye mean.
498 **ferde as** acted as if.
    deye die.
500 **echon** all, each one.
501 **trewe, verray** faithful, true. Alison speaks about her fidelity while we know she is planning to be unfaithful. This might result in comic irony or it might undermine the meaning of the word 'truth'. (Compare with line 283.)
503–5 John's emotion (*affeccioun*) for Alison overwhelms his reason, in the same way that something may be so strongly present in someone's imagination (*ymaginacioun*) that they act (in the

extreme case even dying) as if it were real. Is the Miller also implying that John has a strong imagination? What is the tone of voice here?

503 **which** what.

505 Such a deep impression (*impressioun*) may be recorded (within it). Medieval discussions of the workings of the mind often compared the trace of an object or concept in the memory and imagination to an impression made in wax.

506 **quake** tremble.

507 It seems to him that he can truly (*verraily*) see. He worries about the flood so powerfully and vividly that he thinks it is actually happening.

508 **walwynge** rolling, surging.

509 **drenchen** drown. Does John's anxiety prove the strength of his affection for Alison, or does it make him ridiculous?

510 **maketh sory cheere** looks miserable.

511 **sory swogh** wretched groan.

514–15 Notice the further repetitions of *pryvely, pryvetee*, poking fun at John's belief in the secrecy of his actions, but also questioning the meaning of the word.

516 **His owene hand** with his own hand. So that no one should wonder why he wants three ladders.

517 **stalkes** uprights, as opposed to rungs (*ronges*).

518 **in the balkes** among the, or from the, beams.

519 **hem vitailled** provisioned them, stored food in them.

520 **jubbe** jug.

521 **Suffisynge** sufficient.

522 **array** preparation.

523 **wenche** womanservant.

524 **Upon his nede** on his business. The journey to London would take at least two days in each direction.

John awaits the flood; Nicholas takes over his bed: lines 525–48

After a long day of preparation, John, Alison and Nicholas climb into their three tubs, say their prayers and wait for the flood.

When John is asleep, Alison and Nicholas climb back down their ladders and go together to John's bed, where they make love until the early morning. The Miller emphasizes the pompous religiosity (lines 530–4) and the exhaustion (lines 535–9) of John the carpenter, and sets them against the discretion (lines 540–2) and the pleasure (lines 544–6) of the young couple. Do we feel sorry for John, or is it inevitable that Alison and Nicholas will enjoy each other in his bed while, lying in his tub, he dreams of salvation and power? What is the effect of the visual image (John in his tub among the rafters, the lovers in his bed below) which Chaucer and the Miller have created?

525 **whan it drow to nyght**   when it was nearly dark, at dusk.

526 Presumably candles were usually left burning, but John wants to give the impression that no one is ready to answer the door.

528 **clomben**   climbed.

529 **wel a furlong way**   a few minutes, at least the time it would take to walk a furlong (an eighth of a mile, just over 200 metres), which would be less than three minutes.

530 'Now say The Lord's Prayer and then be quiet (*clom*)', said Nicholas.

532 **devocioun**   devotion, prayer.

533 **biddeth**   prays, requests. Perhaps he repeats 'Our Father' and then adds another prayer of his own, or perhaps *devocioun* (line 532) indicates some longer sequence of prayers and praises which the carpenter (always?) says. Do you regard John as a religious person, or is he trying to live up to the role of Noah?

534 **it heere**   might hear it.

535 **dede sleep**   a very deep sleep.
   for wery bisynesse   because of the exertions of his activity, but the sense of 'wearied by his worries' may also be present.

537 **moore**   later. Curfew time (*corfew-tyme*), the time of a bell which signalled that domestic fires should be covered and people return to their houses, was about eight o'clock in the evening.

538 He groans deeply because of the suffering (*travaille*) of his spirit (*goost*).

539 **routeth**   snores.
   myslay   was lying awkwardly.

540 **stalketh** creeps.

541 **ful... spedde** went down quickly and quietly.

543 **Ther as** where.

544 **revel** merriment.

545 **lith** lie.

546 Occupied (*In bisynesse*) with enjoyment (*mirthe*) and delight (*solas*).

547 **laudes** lauds, a church service which took place some time before dawn. Notice the different kinds of music here. (See p. 140.)

    gan to rynge began to ring.

548 **freres** friars. Only monks and friars would have to attend lauds.

    chauncel chancel, area of the church in front of the main altar.

Absolon decides to speak to Alison at her window: lines 549–78

Absolon concludes that John has gone on a business trip and decides to take advantage of his absence by making another visit to Alison's bedroom window, to confess his love to her and, he hopes, to receive a kiss in return. We learn about the way Absolon has been watching John's door (lines 565–6), and enquiring of the monks about his whereabouts (lines 553–62). But Absolon is also a practical lover. His suffering for love (line 550) does not prevent him from enjoying the company of his friends (line 552). He decides to stay awake all night like a lover (line 564) but goes home to sleep first (line 577). We also learn more about John's working habits, his absences from home, and the trust the Abbey places in his judgement (lines 557–60). What is the effect of giving this information at this point?

552 **hym to disporte** to enjoy himself.

553 **upon cas** by chance.

    cloisterer monk (one of the monks of Osney Abbey, presumably).

554 **after** about.

555 **drough hym apart**   took him aside. Again the emphasis is on
secrecy. Presumably Absolon and his friends went into the
Abbey church, where Absolon happened to meet a monk he
knew who took him outside to answer his question. As with
the lauds bell (line 547), and the pilgrimage itself, there is an
interesting mingling and separation of secular pleasure and
religious observance around the church. Absolon finds his
informant inside the church and asks the leading question
there, but the monk prefers to answer privately outside.

556 **noot**   (= *ne woot*) do not know.

557 **Syn**   since. The implication is that John has work to do at the
Abbey almost every day.
trowe   think, believe.

558 **ther**   wherever. It would be usual for someone responsible for
a large building to send a carpenter to a wood (which might be
at some distance and might belong to the Abbey) to select
timber for repairs or additions. While they were away they
would stay at the *grange* (line 560), a farm building or granary
which would be part of the Abbey estate.

561 The monk tells Nicholas that John must either be away or at his
own house. Since Nicholas has not seen John at home, he
reasons that he must be away, even though his informant said
he had no certain knowledge (line 562).

562 **soothly**   truly.

563 **joly**   lively, sprightly (this adjective is often used of Absolon).
light   cheerful, glad.

565 **stirynge**   moving.

566 **sprynge**   break.

567 **So moot I thryve**   As I may prosper (a common exclamation).

568 How do you understand *pryvely* here? (Compare with other
references to secrecy in lines 554, 514 and 56.)

569 Which stands low down on his bedroom wall (*boures wal*).

571 **I shal nat mysse**   I shall not fail.

572 **leeste**   least.

573 **parfay**   by my faith (a common light exclamation).

574 **icched**   itched. Is this ironic in view of line 626?

576 **me mette**   I dreamed (presumably this was on Sunday night).
feeste   feast. Perhaps this is an ironic reference back to the
lovers' *revel* (line 544).

577 If Absolon has an early evening nap he will be better able to
stay up all night. But how does this practicality place Absolon
in relation to the love convention he is trying to follow? Noble
lovers stay up all night because they are too anxious to sleep.
Absolon sleeps much longer than he intends (line 579).

578 **pleye** frolic, amuse myself (the word also has a sexual sense
which may be ironic here, since as Absolon sleeps Nicholas and
Alison *pleye*).

Absolon goes to the window and confesses his love: lines 579–605

Just before dawn, much later than he intended, Absolon wakes
up and prepares himself to address Alison. When he speaks to
her in the elaborate language of the lover, she tells him plainly
that she has another lover, and that he should go away and let her
sleep. Absolon prepares thoroughly, taking particular care that
his breath should smell sweet (lines 582–5). He hopes that the
kiss he has set his heart on will be the first of many, and he wants
Alison to enjoy it. Is this considerate or ridiculous? His language
(which may refer to The Song of Solomon, a book of the Bible,
which describes God's love of the Church in the form of a love-
poem) evokes the sweet herbs he has chewed (lines 590–91) and
the animal imagery (lines 591, 596–8) associated with Alison
earlier (lines 126, 150–5, 174). Does the language suit his station
and emotions? (See p. 130.) What do you make of the contrast
with the language of her reply (lines 600–05)?

579 Presumably (see line 623) the first cock crows some time before
dawn. But still Absolon has slept most of the night, whereas
Nicholas and Alison, who were making love until lauds, have
been asleep only for an hour or two. Perhaps this suggests a
contrast between the (theoretical) wakefulness of the courtly
lover and the more practical wakefulness of Nicholas, the
successful lover. (Compare also with lines 247–9.)

580 **rist**   rose.

581 And dresses himself (*arraieth*) handsomely (*gay*) to the last detail (*poynt-devys*).

582 **greyn**   cardomom seed, a hot sweet-smelling spice. Nicholas's natural sweetness is compared to liquorice (line 99).

584 **trewe-love**   herb paris (called a true love because the shape of its four leaves resembles a love-knot), carried (*beer*) for the smell (or perhaps for the name).

585 **gracious**   pleasing, attractive.

586 **rometh**   makes his way (perhaps an ironic use of a courtly word).

588 **Unto... raughte**   it reached only up to his chest. Or perhaps a little below, since when Absolon kneels his face is level with the window (line 615).

589 **semy soun**   small or soft sound.

590 **What do ye**   How are you? Absolon uses the submissive, polite pronoun.

590–1 Honey-comb (*hony-comb*) and cinnamon (*cynamome*) are both terms of affection found in The Song of Solomon 4:11 and 14.

591 **bryd**   bird. Absolon uses the vocabulary of popular lovesongs.

592 **Awaketh**   wake up (imperative form).

593 **Wel litel**   very little.

594 **I swete ther I go**   I sweat wherever I go. Absolon interprets it as a sign of love, but Alison may find this characteristic off-putting.

595 It is no wonder if I melt (*swelte*) and sweat.

596 **moorne**   mourn.

    tete   teat.

598 **turtel**   turtle-dove.

599 Absolon means to say that his appetite is much reduced because of love (which would be a typical symptom of courtly love), but he ends up saying that he eats the same as a young girl.

600 **Go fro**   go away from. Presumably Jack fool is an expression of contempt.

601 **"com pa me"**   come kiss me (possibly the words were from a popular song).

602 Would she be at fault (*to blame*) if she did not have another lover whom she loved better than Absolon? Or is she pretending to refer to her husband?

604 What does this threat tell us about her opinion of Absolon?

605 **a twenty devel wey**   in the name of twenty devils.

Alison puts her bottom out of the window: lines 606–35

Absolon agrees to go away in return for a kiss. For her amusement and Nicholas's, Alison puts her bottom out of the window. When Absolon kisses what he takes to be her face, he is at first surprised at her beard, but then realizes the mistake he has made, to much laughter from the lovers. This is the first climax of the story, and it is worth observing how Chaucer keeps in play the separate voices (and outlooks) of his three characters alongside his narrative voice and the dominating visual image of the would-be lover kneeling in the dark and kissing whatever emerges from the window. In the other versions of this story which we have (and which we assume Chaucer worked from) it is the successful male lover who bares his bottom. What are the advantages (for the story) of Alison conceiving and carrying out this insulting joke? Do you think Absolon deserves to have this trick played on him? (See pp. 129–31 and 154–5.)

607 **so yvel biset**   so badly misplaced (or possibly, so badly mistreated). Absolon continues to flatter himself that he is a true lover.

608 **syn... bet**   since it cannot turn out any better.

610 **Wiltow**   (= *wilt thow*) will you.

611 **certes**   certainly.

614 **hust**   hush, be quiet. Alison's action could be interpreted mainly as a lesson for Absolon or mainly as a joke to be shared with Nicholas. How does this relate to the idea of sharing secrets/*pryvetee* in the tale? (It is worth noting that some good early manuscripts omit lines 613–14, but most editors think Chaucer wrote them.)

615 **doun sette hym**   got down. He has to do this because the

window is so low (if the window were higher Alison's trick would not work), but it adds to the humorous visual symbolism (the courtly lover on his knees to his mistress), and to his humiliation, that Absolon should be kneeling.

616 **at alle degrees**   in every way (perhaps, at every stage). In either case Absolon thinks he is managing his affair successfully, imagining that what Alison sees as a goodbye kiss will actually be the first of many (line 617).

618 Sweetheart, give me your favour (*grace*) and sweet bird, your mercy (*oore*).

619 **undoth**   undoes, opens.

620 'Have done', she said, 'hurry up, and be quick.' Hurrying him seems to be a way of dominating Absolon. This is one of Nicholas's techniques.

622 **gan wype**   wiped.

623 **pich**   pitch.

624 Is it the rhyme or the word order that makes this line so funny?

625 **hym... wers**   nothing better or worse happened to him (that is, exactly this happened).

626 **But**   than.
   ers   arse. The very coarse vocabulary of the narration reflects the actions here and contrasts with Absolon's language.

627 **Ful savourly**   with relish, carefully registering the taste and smell.

628 **Abak he stirte**   he started, or jumped, back. When Chaucer writes 'he thought there was something wrong', is this comic understatement or are we watching Absolon's (rather slow) mind in action?

629 **wiste**   knew. How does mentioning the beard increase the humour?

630 **long yherd**   long-haired.

631 *Fy* and *allas* are both exclamations, but the sequence is important. Absolon feels contempt and anger, and then sorrow (for himself).
   do   done.

632 **clapte**   slammed. How does *Tehee* add to our sense of Alison's personality?

633 **a sory pas**   with sad steps. Is Absolon wiser now?

634 Some critics see a pun here: the first beard is literal, the second

a metaphorical sense meaning 'joke'. It may be a problem that
Nicholas has to overhear Absolon's thought about Alison's
'beard'. What does *hende* mean here (see Note to line 91, p. 52)?

635 **corpus** (Latin) body.

faire and weel marvellously. Does Nicholas appreciate Alison
better now?

Absolon learns his lesson and plans his revenge: lines 636–77

As Absolon hears the mocking laughter of Alison and Nicholas he
realizes the depth of his humiliation. Anger and disgust give way
to thoughts of revenge. He walks across the street to a blacksmith's
forge and borrows a red hot plough-blade. The passage contrasts
the physicality of Absolon's attempts to clean his mouth (lines
639–40) with his mental anguish (lines 641–51), the labour of the
smithy (lines 654–5) with the realistic social exchange (lines 656–
76). Absolon may be humiliated in the semi-private world of the
love triangle but he has a network of acquaintances who are more
than ready to exchange favours with him.

636 **sely** hapless, unfortunate.

every deel every part, every word.

637 To bite one's lip was a conventional indication of anger in
Middle English. There may also be special reasons why
Absolon bit his.

638 Why do you think Absolon switches to the intimate pronoun
(*thee*) now? (Compare with line 590 and see A Note on
Chaucer's English, pp. 175–6.)

639 **froteth** rubs, chafes. The sentence is a rhetorical question:
who now rubs his mouth but Absolon?

640 **sond** sand.

chippes woodchips.

642 May I give my soul to Satan. The sentence is conditional. May
I give my soul to Satan if I would not rather be avenged
than…

643–4 If I would not rather (*levere*) be avenged (*awroken*) for this insult (*despit*) than own this whole town, he said.

645 What a pity that I did not avoid (*ybleynt*) it.

646 **yqueynt** quenched.

648 He did not consider love (*paramours*) worth anything (*kers* means cress).

649 Is he cured of love or of the sickness of seeing himself and others in a false light?

650 **gan deffie** denounced. Not only has he finished with love himself, but he tries to warn others against it. Perhaps Absolon continues to make himself ridiculous.

651 **weep** wept.

652 **A softe paas he wente** he walked quietly (or perhaps slowly). What is the significance of Absolon's quiet calmness here and later (line 656)?

653 To (*Until*) a blacksmith whom people called master Gervase. Blacksmiths did virtually all metalwork as well as shoeing horses. Their shops would be at work early in the morning, making, sharpening and repairing implements required for the day's work.

654 **smythed** made, or repaired.
plough harneys ploughing gear.

655 **sharpeth** sharpens. The Miller mentions metal parts of the plough. The coulter (*kultour*) is an iron blade which cuts the earth vertically. It is placed in front of the share (*shaar*) which horizontally splits apart the earth above the coulter and lifts it to the side.

659 **for Cristes sweete tree** by Christ's blessed cross.

660 **rathe** early.
benedicitee bless me.

661 **gay gerl** amorous girl (perhaps with an implication of immorality). Like Absolon, Gervase associates early mornings with love.

662 This is the only known occurrence of the word *viritoot* and no one really knows what it means. The most common explanation is 'on the move' or 'astir'. But perhaps it should be part of Gervase's rude banter, possibly as a colloquial expression which was never otherwise recorded in a written source.

663 St Neot (*Note*) was an Anglo-Saxon saint of the ninth century,

about whom very little is known. There are legends associating him with Oxford.

664 **ne roghte nat a bene**   did not care a bean.

665 **no word agayn he yaf**   he did not say a word in reply.

666 **tow**   flax. A distaff (*distaf*) is an implement used in spinning thread. But this expression is a proverb meaning 'to have business in hand'.

668 **chymenee**   fireplace, hearth.

669 Lend it me; I have something to do with it.

670 **agayn**   back.

672 **poke**   bag.

nobles alle untold   uncounted, countless gold coins (compare with line 148).

673 **Thou sholdest have**   you should have it. His conversations with Gervase show us another side to Absolon's character, placing his former courtly pretensions in a context of ordinary working life.

674 **Ey, Cristes foo!**   By the Devil.

675 **be as be may**   be that as it may. For the present Absolon will give no explanations.

676 **to-morwe day**   another time.

677 **caughte**   picked up.

stele   handle.

Absolon's revenge: lines 678–705

With the plough-coulter in hand, Absolon goes to the window and begs another kiss, offering Alison a gold ring if she agrees. To complete the joke Nicholas puts his bottom out of the window and lets fly a fart. But his joke turns against him in the second climax of the story. Instead of a kiss he receives the red-hot coulter which burns the skin all around his bottom. Each character in this passage aims to mislead the person they address and is in turn misled by the reply. But the comedy of misunderstanding turns physical with Nicholas's fart and Absolon's hot knife. Even the latter is misdirected, since

Absolon intends to take revenge on Alison. (See p. 131.)

678 **gan to stele**   crept out.

683 **warante**   swear, wager.

684 **leef**   beloved (see line 285). Absolon's language and his offer seem very suspicious. Why do the lovers not suspect his plan?

687 **yaf**   gave.

688 **therto wel ygrave**   also beautifully engraved.

689 **yeve**   give. Absolon uses polite thou-forms to stress his humility.

690 **was risen**   had got up.

691 **amended al the jape**   improve the joke. Nicholas may make his extraordinary mistake because he now has complete contempt for Absolon, or because he is trying to compete with Alison.

693 Presumably the window is hinged at the top.

694 How does *pryvely* function here?

695 **Over**   beyond.

696 **therwith**   at that. At the second climax of the poem Chaucer reminds us that both Absolon and Nicholas are clerks.

697 **I noot nat**   I do not know. This sentence combines love-flattery with practicality: Absolon needs a sound to aim at. Why does Alison not answer? Does she see through his trick?

698 **leet fle**   let fly.

699 **thonder-dent**   thunderclap. Perhaps we should remember Nicholas's storm.

700 **yblent**   blinded.

701 **iren hoot**   hot iron implement.

702 **smoot**   struck.

703 **Of**   off.

   an hande-brede about   a hand's breadth around.

704 **toute**   buttocks.

705 **smert**   pain. In what ways is this extremely painful punishment appropriate for Nicholas?

John's fall and the reaction of his neighbours: lines 706–46

Nicholas shouts for water to treat his burns. His cries wake John who, thinking that the flood has come, cuts his tub loose from the rafters. He falls straight to the floor and knocks himself out. Alison and Nicholas run out into the street shouting, at which the neighbours come in and stare at John. The lovers' version of events is accepted by the town and he is ridiculed as a madman. The Miller ends by listing the penalties paid by the three men.

What does Chaucer do to keep his third climax a surprise? It is possible to see the way the three stories (the flood, the kiss, the branding) interact as humorous coincidence, but it may be an example of the way in which a greater design can operate through the stratagems and mistakes of individual characters. Should we regard this as God's plan working in the world, or is it at best 'poetic justice'?

Why are John's neighbours introduced at the end of the tale? Perhaps there is a connection between the way Nicholas uses the story of the flood to trick John (lines 405–54) and the way he successfully rewrites the tale to his own advantage at the end (lines 716–41). We may feel sympathy for John as the victim of Nicholas's imagination and reinterpretation.

707   **herte**   heart. The sacred heart (of Jesus) was an object of veneration in the Middle Ages, but in Nicholas's state any oath will do.

708   **sterte**   awoke, leaped.

709   **oon**   someone.

710   *Nowelis* is John's dim recollection of Noah's name (compare with line 429), with a little help from Christmas.

711   **He sit hym**   he sat. Is it significant for the rest of the tale that John says no more (*mo*) words here?

713   **foond**   tried.
      selle   sell. The general meaning is that he fell directly to the ground, without having time to do anything. Editors usually

explain Chaucer's use of this phrase by referring to a similar phrase ('and while he was falling he did not find any bread to sell') in *Aloul*, an Old French *fabliau*. Bread and ale were already in the tub. This may be the best we can do, but I wish there was something better, especially in view of the awkward repetition in lines 714–15.

714 **celle** floor.

715 **aswowne** in a faint, unconscious.

716 **stirte hire** jumped. While John is unconscious the two lovers ensure that their version of events is heard first. Nicholas is already out of bed.

718 **smale and grete** poor and rich (that is, everyone).

719 **In ronnen** run in.

 gauren on stare at.

720 *Wan* is another word for pale.

721 **brosten** broken. What would breaking his arm mean to John the carpenter?

722 Do you take *stonde* (stand) literally ('he must get up') or metaphorically ('he must take responsibility' or 'he must face up to')?

 unto to, for, in spite of (depending on how *stonde* is understood).

723 **bore doun** overcome, contradicted.

724 **With** by. Is *hende* simply sarcastic here?

726 **agast so** so afraid. (For *Nowelis* see Note to line 710, p. 96.) Apparently they overhear John's thought.

727 **fantasie** imagination (or perhaps, delusion). Which seems better to you? It would make sense to have a comma after *fantasie*.

 vanytee foolishness. How do Alison's and Nicholas's choice of words distort the story we have heard? Can you think of fairer words?

728 **yboght hym** bought himself.

731 *par compaignye* to keep him company. How does the use of a French phrase here, and the reference to God (line 730), add to the sense of ridicule? Compare the other uses of *compaignye* in the tale (lines 96, 552).

732 **fantasye** delusion.

733 Notice how the people now stare in amazement at John's

actions using the same words with which Nicholas tricked him at lines 335–6.

734 Compare with line 282, where all Absolon's *ernest* is made into a joke. In defending his choice of tale the Miller upheld the related proposition that jokes should not be taken seriously (line 78). This interest in the exchanges between jest and *ernest* is very characteristic of Chaucer. Might we take this line as inviting some sympathy for John?

735 **what so**   whatever.

736 **reson**   reason(s), explanations. A very strong way of expressing the frustration of John's situation. What is the state of John's reason if no one pays attention to his version of events? But his experience of failing to make sense corresponds to something real in the tale. There seems to be a rational explanation given for everything that happens, yet so much of it is weird and fantastical.

737 **sworn adoun**   overcome (or silenced) by what they swore to. Compare with the Modern English phrase 'shouted down'. What does it mean that John is overcome by their strong oaths (*othes grete*) rather than their reasons?

738 **holde wood**   considered mad. Why *holde*? Why might being treated as a madman by his neighbours be a suitable punishment for John? (Compare with line 452.)

739 For all the men of learning immediately sided with their fellow. Here *clerk* must refer to the teachers (and perhaps the priests) as well as the students. This line increases our feeling that people are conspiring against John.

741 **stryf**   quarrel, commotion.

742 Polite editors (the majority) gloss *swyved* as 'copulated with', but 'screwed' gives a better idea of the tone. Notice that the verb is in the passive here. Is this part of John's public humiliation or something that only the lovers know? Which of the three penalties paid by John (being cuckolded, breaking his arm, being treated as a madman) would be most painful to him?

743 **For al his kepyng**   in spite of all his guarding.

744 **nether ye**   anus (literally, lower eye).

746 Is the Miller's blessing affected by the line it rhymes with?

The Reeve's Prologue

Reaction to *The Miller's Tale*

The main purpose of *The Reeve's Prologue* is to introduce *The Reeve's Tale* by presenting the Reeve's intention and preoccupations. But we also learn how the pilgrims in general, and the Reeve in particular, reacted to *The Miller's Tale*. We are told that many of them laughed (line 747), that different people reacted differently (line 749), that most of them took it light-heartedly (line 750), and that only the Reeve was really upset. How does this compare with the reaction to *The Knight's Tale* (lines 1–5)? Might you have expected more reaction?

The Reeve's intervention in *The Miller's Prologue* (lines 36–41) has already prepared us for his angry response. Now he explains that he resents the slur against carpenters (lines 753, 806), that he would like revenge (lines 756, 803–08), and that he is old (line 759). Is the Reeve's description of the vices of old men (lines 760–90) a reason for not taking revenge (line 759), a fragment of autobiography, or an explanation of the depth of his feelings? Do you think it reasonable that the Reeve should regard *The Miller's Tale* as a personal attack on him?

747 **nyce**   foolish.
751 **hym greve**   become angry.
754–5 *Litel* and *lite* may be ironic understatement.
755 **gan to grucche**   complained.
756 **So theek**   (= *so thee ik*) as I may prosper.
757 **bleryng... ye**   (a tale of) deceiving a proud miller, literally dimming his eye.
759 **me... age**   I do not wish to joke because of my age. Or perhaps he means that he has no wish to tell a tale, but he seems keen enough later.
760 The Reeve imagines himself as an old horse, who no longer eats grass in the field, but whose only food (*fodder*) is dry winter food (*forage*) in the stable.

761   **writeth**   declares, signifies.

762   **mowled**   gone mouldy. His white hairs (*white top*) are now envisaged as fibres of mould growing out of his head.

763   The fruit of the medlar tree was called an open-arse (*open-ers*) on account of its appearance, and was usually eaten when it was almost rotten.

765   **mullok**   rubbish.

      stree   straw.

768   **hoppen**   dance.

      pype   play a tune.

769   **wyl**   will, wishes (with a strong sexual overtone, brought out in line 770).

      ther... nayl   one desire always remains, sharp as a nail.

770   **hoor**   grey-haired.

      grene tayl   youthful, vigorous sexual organ.

772   **evere in oon**   continually.

773   How do you reconcile this line with his earlier remark that age would prevent him from engaging in a contest of ribaldry (lines 758–9)? Might it be that he takes a grimmer, less amused view of sexual desire than the Miller?

774   **asshen olde**   old ashes.

      yreke   covered over (but still present).

775   **gleedes**   glowing coals. In making this division of vices the Reeve imitates the methods of medieval preachers.

776   **Avauntyng**   boasting.

      coveitise   covetousness, strong desire for possessions, especially (but not only) those belonging to other people.

777   **longen**   belong.

      eelde   old age.

778   **lemes**   limbs.

      unweelde   feeble, unwieldy.

780   **a coltes tooth**   the desires of a young man. This is a proverbial expression, but notice that the Reeve again uses an image connected to horses.

781   **henne**   hence, away.

782–7   The Reeve employs an extended metaphor from the handling of wine-barrels. The tap (*tappe*) was a thick tapered stick pushed into the tap-hole (also known as the tap as in line 785) to close the barrel (*tonne* [line 786]), and removed to allow the wine to flow out. The barrel was placed on its side, so that when it was first opened the wine poured out vigorously. Later on, the flow reduced to a trickle, when the wine might drip onto the rim (*chymbe* [line 787]) of the barrel. The Reeve compares this gradual loss of vigour to his experience of life, and particularly to his sexual capability. The idea that decay is implicit even in youth is brought out by the image of Death (*Deeth* [line 784]) as the tapster who first pulled out the tap (*drough the tappe* [line 784]) when the Reeve was born (*bore* [line 783]).

788 **chymbe**   chime.

789 **ful yoore**   long ago.

790 Old people have nothing left except the folly of age (*dotage*).

793 **amounteth**   amount to.

794 **hooly writ**   scripture.

796 **soutere**   cobbler.

leche   doctor.

798 **Lo Depeford**   Here is Deptford (then a village about 6 km from Southwark).

half-wey pryme   about 6.30 am.

799 **Grenewych**   Greenwich (about 1 km further on their journey). Probably Chaucer was living there in the 1390s. The reference to rogues (*many a shrewe*) should be taken as a self-deprecating joke.

803 **sette his howve**   tip his hood, make him look a fool.

804 It is allowed (*leveful*) to repel (*of-showve*) force with force.

807 **Peraventure**   perhaps.

809 **cherles termes**   rude words.

810 **to-breke**   be broken apart.

812 **balke**   beam. The Reeve is alluding to the sermon on the mount, where Jesus castigates hypocrites who can detect small faults in others but are blind to much larger faults in themselves. (See Matthew 7:3.)

A fifeenth-century engraving showing Sir Launcelot kneeling before
Queen Guinevere in her chamber

Interpretations

The Miller as a character and contrasts with the Knight

At the end of the *General Prologue*, when Harry Bailly, the Host, proposes the storytelling competition, he asks the Knight to tell the first tale after lots have been drawn. This is fitting because the Knight has the highest rank and status in medieval society and is likely to set a certain tone by telling an elegant story. The Knight obliges with a fitting tale of courtly romance full of classical heroism and nobility. We learned of the Knight's nobility in the portrait in *The General Prologue*: he was *a very parfit gentil knight*.

In *The Knight's Tale*, there are descriptions in vivid detail of the temples of Venus, Mars and Diana and of the heroic military preparations for the tournament between the rival suitors for Emily's love. It is also a very long tale – the longest of all the verse tales – and the structure is well organized and formal. There are interruptions only for philosophical comment. When the tale is finished and it is time to choose the second storyteller, Harry Bailly understandably turns to the Monk as the next in line of social importance among the pilgrims. He expects the Monk to tell an equally noble story.

> 'Now telleth ye, sir Monk, if that ye konne,
> Somwhat to quite with the Knyghtes tale'   (10–11)

Then, all of a sudden, the Miller insists on telling the second tale, and, using an arrogant and assertive tone, it is clear that he intends to get his way. As is the case with many other tales in the collection, we can detect a link between tale and teller, and if we look back at the *General Prologue* we can find evidence of the pilgrim's character in the original pen portrait. In his portrait the Miller is described as a larger-than-life character who loves buffoonery and indecent stories. He is unscrupulous, dishonest in temperament and brawny of appearance. These characteristics appear to be further developed through his intimidating and overpowering behaviour in *The Miller's Prologue* when he rides roughshod over all other views and insists on his right to tell his story. He also reveals without shame that he is drunk and he picks an argument with the Reeve, who, like John in the tale we are to hear, is a carpenter.

Activity

Look at the words exchanged between the Miller and the Host (lines 20–35) and those between the Miller and the Reeve (lines 36–58). Reread the portrait of the Miller from the *General Prologue*. Can you see how characteristics of the Miller are further developed in his Prologue?

Discussion

In the *General Prologue*, we learn that the Miller could break doors off their hinges or charge them down with his head. He exhibits great strength at wrestling matches. Consider his physical appearance: he has a huge beard, wide nostrils, a vast mouth and a conspicuous wart, crowned by a tuft of hairs like the bristles of a sow's ears. By stressing the Miller's physical attributes, Chaucer suggests to the reader the idea of a down-to-earth man who takes pleasure in satisfying basic appetites. Now we learn that he is drunk. As well as sitting awkwardly on his horse, he speaks in *Pilates voys* (line 16) and admits to his own inebriation:

> 'But first I make a protestacioun
> That I am dronke; I knowe it by my soun.' (29–30)

He is also very forceful, insisting on standing his ground: *'For I wol speke or elles go my wey'* (line 25). The Host is moved to warn that, in his opinion, the Miller's *wit is overcome* (line 27).

But *The Miller's Prologue* does more than simply extend our understanding of his appearance and character. It is more complicated. Remember that Chaucer himself has a role in the prologue. (It is actually always interesting to reflect on Chaucer's role in the poem, bearing in mind that there is a very real sense in which all the words spoken are done so by Chaucer, the poet.) Near the end of the *General Prologue*, Chaucer gives an elaborate apology for having to report directly what he heard on the journey. In a way he was saying: don't blame me for the stories I have to tell as I am only reporting them. If that was the first hint we got of Chaucer's disingenuousness – a sort of innocent craftiness – we probably see it again here in *The Miller's Prologue*. Notice that Chaucer (as the character or voice of the pilgrim) somewhat characteristically stands back from the conversations between the Host, the Reeve and the Miller.

The Miller is going to tell a bawdy story about the 'cuckolding' of a husband, which will contrast with the previous tale (the Knight's), and which could potentially make fun of the Reeve. The Miller's comments on the fidelity (sexual loyalty) of wives ironically casts doubt on the Reeve's marriage while giving no explicit cause for offence. Having presented all this neutrally, Chaucer now introduces his own comment. In the guise of the pilgrim, he apologizes for the forthcoming tale that he must report, much as he apologized earlier in the *General Prologue*.

You will see that the Miller, during the justification of the tale, speaks with double meanings of a sexual nature – ultimately this is Chaucer's choice of language – particularly centred on the word *pryvetee* (line 56), meaning both 'secrets' and 'private parts' or 'genitals'. (See Notes, p. 46.) Perhaps Chaucer wants us to imagine that many of the pilgrims will have had their appetites whetted for the sexual behaviour that is about to follow in the tale.

Having listened to the Miller's conversations with the Host and the Reeve, Chaucer pretends to be lost for words: '*What sholde I moore seyn...*' (line 59). Can you see how Chaucer has cleverly used the character and voice of the Miller? Very soon after the initial apology that he made in the *General Prologue* and following just one honourable and noble tale (the Knight's), offensive language, just as he has hinted, will now have to be used to tell a tale that the Host has agreed to. Consider the last section of *The Miller's Prologue* (lines 59–78): the reader is told to *Turne over the leef and chese another tale* (line 69) if he or she is likely to be offended.

My reaction is to do the opposite! Through the character of the Miller, Chaucer has tempted his readers to read on. As well as revealing more about the Miller's character – which might also tempt pilgrim and reader – he has disclaimed responsibility for the sort of language that is going to be spoken, blaming it instead on the Miller.

This disclaimer is important as it frees Chaucer from the burden of responsibility and allows him the freedom to indulge in his wit and versatility.

Genre

The genre of the tale is *fabliau*. Having prepared the pilgrims for a bawdy tale, the Miller proceeds to tell his story about the 'cuckolding' (see Notes pp. 44–5) of John, the carpenter using a range of styles of language, some of which is earthy and crude, about events which themselves are down to earth and crude.

Derek Pearsall (*The Canterbury Tales*, p. 173) suggests that one reason for choosing *fabliau* as a genre is that Chaucer was able to reflect in the tale the reality of experience in life. Although courtly romance, as it appeared in *The Knight's Tale*, could reflect certain aspects of life, the *fabliau* could help him to create a more realistic story, dealing with experience in a different way. Noble and heroic actions in many a courtly romance would have presented love as idealistic and serious; *fabliaux* would have dwelt more on the comic and realistic events in the affairs of love, and many *fabliaux* were also erotic.

Chaucer borrowed from the French and Flemish traditions of *fabliau* and developed many new features of his own. The original features of the genre are summarized in the Notes on pp. 49–50 and other contemporary examples can be found in the Appendix on pp. 196–8. Chaucer added a lot more to the basic elements of *fabliau*.

In an attempt to understand how Chaucer extends the *fabliau* genre, it is always important to bear in mind the contrasts with

The Knight's Tale. Although the genre of *The Miller's Tale* is essentially *fabliau*, there are many elements of courtly romance, in both style and action, similar to the story just told by the Knight. Certain features of the tale suggest that, through the Miller, Chaucer may be parodying a courtly romance. Both the Knight's and the Miller's tales depict conquests of love, and the etiquette (commonly expected behaviour) of courtly love appears in both, although in a very serious way in the Knight's tale and farcically in the Miller's through Absolon's odd pursuit of Alison. In a way, these two tales occupy extremes of settings in life: from the Knight, the noble fantasy of life as it ought to be, in an idealized classical setting; from the Miller, life in its everyday world in a familiar setting in and among the real world where people have to eat, drink, work, sleep, and even perform bodily functions. In one we see the field where Emily celebrates May morning and the temples of Venus, Mars and Diana; in the other, the characters are inhabiting a world where we can almost find our way around John's house, where characters come and go in the local parish, the carpenter goes to buy wood, Nicholas rises to relieve himself and the blacksmith is at work early in his forge.

The similarities with *The Knight's Tale* can be recognized through the distorted conventions of courtly love. In *The Knight's Tale* amorous courtly behaviour seems apt and plausible, and the characters never lose status or dignity as a result of what they do. In *The Miller's Tale*, Absolon's attempts at the conventions of courtly romantic behaviour are utterly ridiculed and he is diminished as a character as a result. As we will see, Absolon, as well as being ridiculous to the audience for the story, is mocked by both Alison and Nicholas, and indirectly by the blacksmith, Gerveys. The more he tries to play the part of a courtly lover, the more ridiculous he appears. A second similarity with *The Knight's Tale* is the rivalry of two suitors (men competing for the attention of one woman) and a third is the downfall of the triumphant hero. In *The Knight's Tale* this is presented as tragic for Arcite, but in *The Miller's*

Tale it is comic and farcical, although nevertheless painful for Nicholas when he is branded by the coulter. Some commentators have also noticed that the Miller copies a stylistic feature of the Knight by switching from simple narration to moralizing, for example:

> Lo, which a greet thyng is affeccioun!
> Men may dyen of ymaginacioun,
> So depe may impressioun be take.   (503–5)

We have to remember that while this was acceptable from the Knight because of his stature and credibility in medieval society, it was questionable from the Miller because he was such a rogue.

Activity

Reread the section in the Notes on *Fabliau*. (See pp. 49–50.) Read the two examples of other *fabliaux* in the Appendix. (See pp. 196–8.) List the features of *fabliau* that Chaucer has used in *The Miller's Tale*. What has Chaucer added to these features? Look at the events, the characters and the language.

Discussion

The examples from other *fabliaux* and the Notes in this book should help you to get some sense of what *fabliau* offered as a genre. You will have noticed that the stories in this tradition contained many elements that are unmistakeably part of *The Miller's Tale*. Your list of recognizable features probably includes deception, misdeed, sex and excretion, the presence of a jealous older husband and lecherous student, and the theme of victimization. These themes and characters were well suited to Chaucer's form of oral (spoken) storytelling, which copes well with ordinary life in down-to-earth settings.

    The Miller's Tale is not the only Canterbury Tale to use the genre of *fabliau*. An interesting idea, suggested by the critic, D.S. Brewer, in his essay, *The Fabliaux* (see Rowland, 1968) is that Chaucer's examples of the form are marked out by their mixture of styles: courtly and romantic on the one hand, realistic or naturalistic on the other. It is also often noted that Chaucer added a lot of characterization. This approach gave his *fabliaux* a richness and complexity that would not have been present in many others, which were simply anecdotes in which the events were mentioned but without developing the characters as possible real people. Having made some comparisons, do you agree that Chaucer succeeded in adding elements in this *fabliau* that made settings, plot, and character all more meaningful?

Do not be too concerned about trying to identify the tale just as *fabliau*. You have already learned that Chaucer adapted the genre by adding other features to it and that he was probably allowing the Miller to tell a story that would contrast with and parody the previous one told by the Knight. He appears also to have taken much further the element of vernacular (everyday language). But as you read the tale and studied the Notes, you will have become aware of another element that was prominent, which perhaps seems out of place in a *fabliau* – that is the religious irony. There are many parts to the religious framework, such as temptations, sin, moral themes and not least the central parody of the story of the Flood and Noah's Ark.

Characterization

Bear in mind that *The Miller's Tale* is really the third section of the whole work known as *The Canterbury Tales*. You have been introduced to *The Knight's Tale*, which comes just before it, and before that there is the *General Prologue*, which is a kind of introduction. Most of the *General Prologue* involves individual descriptions, rather like pen portraits, of each pilgrim. Remember that the Miller was one of a number of the company riding towards Canterbury. These portraits serve not only to introduce the pilgrims, most of whom will later tell a story in the competition on the journey by horseback to Canterbury and back to Southwark, but also to characterize each of them. One by one the pilgrims, who have assembled in the Tabard Inn in Southwark, are described by Chaucer as if he, the poet, were there among them. The portraits vary in length, but the style is similar throughout: economical, often mildly ironic, sometimes more harshly satirical, always witty and perceptive. For a variety of reasons they amount to one of the most celebrated and unique pieces of poetry in English literature. There is often sharp understanding of the motives for human behaviour, exposing vanity, greed and corruption in some characters, while others are charitable and noble. There is a huge array of medieval life on display. Just as he does with the Miller, Chaucer later develops the characters of the pilgrims, sometimes through conversations in between the stories and also through the kinds of stories they are given to tell.

In *The Miller's Tale* a very similar technique is used to introduce the reader to three of the main characters, Nicholas, Alison, and Absolon, and although John is not introduced in quite such a detailed portrait, he too is brought to life between lines 113 and 124, where the Miller deals with his big mistake in marrying someone so different from himself, and comments on his ignorance:

> He knew nat Catoun, for his wit was rude,
> That bad man sholde wedde his simylitude. (119–20)

Nicholas's portrait presents him in marked contrast to the Clerk in the *General Prologue*, who is rather unworldly, a young man of few words, devoted to his study. By contrast *hende* Nicholas plays the psaltery (like a guitar) and perfects his singing voice.

The vivid characterization contrasts with *The Knight's Tale*, in which the lovers had a role to play as part of the romance but were never brought to life as real characters like they are by the Miller. In keeping with the genre of *fabliau*, the characters are to some extent stock types, but they become increasingly individualized through their actions, as the story unfolds.

Activity

How are the four main characters involved in each others' lives?

Discussion

Much of the humour and the themes stem from the various connections between the four main protagonists. Each of them is introduced and presented in a way that identifies the potential cause of their downfall. As we follow their actions, the original character traits described in their introductions are borne out by behaviour that is either foolish or naïve. All of their actions link them together in ways that harm them individually and collectively. To an extent these are the links of 'stock' characters predicted to be found in a *fabliau*.

The jealous, ageing husband who is over-possessive of his younger wife is on the receiving end of an elaborate joke engineered by the clever student who makes a cuckold of him, while the squeamish parish clerk is also made to appear a complete fool by the two clever adulterers. And yet the tables are turned on them by the parish clerk's revengeful scheme, which then leads in turn to the jealous husband's terrible accident when he hears what he believes to be a warning about the arrival of the flood.

Chaucer's sense of structure is acute. There are associations and connections that link all the characters in the plot and there are features in the lives of each main character, which will have a strong bearing on how they are treated by the others. Nicholas's astrology points to the main events of the story and the way in which he will dupe John. When John is introduced there are hints about the significance of the marital age difference that is such a central part of the tale. The flirtatious early relations between Nicholas and Alison are a forerunner of the night of passion they are later to spend with each other. Absolon's squeamishness combined with his determined wooing at the *shot-wyndowe* set him up for the trap that awaits him.

> But sooth to seyn, he was somdeel squaymous
> Of fartyng, and of speche daungerous.   (229–30)

Although their effects on each other are comic, the results are painful or humiliating in ways they could not have predicted, perhaps because of the kinds of characters they are. Themes of punishment and destiny are also linked with what happens to the characters. John's simplicity leads him to believe all of Nicholas's trickery. Nicholas's supreme over-confidence and the thrill he gains from his cuckolding scheme lead him to a painful conclusion and all of Absolon's sexual pretentions and delusions predictably end in complete humiliation. Perhaps only Alison emerges from the web of connected events unscathed, although some critics have suggested that she is more punished than the others simply by not being punished at all; at least not on earth, perhaps having to await her retribution in a later life!

John

John is an example of a stock, or stereotype, character, who later becomes individualized. He is rich, but stupid, and his gullibility provides the chance for the main practical joke of the story. The fact that he has married a younger wife would be difficult enough for any older husband, but it is catastrophic for John who is so naïve and possessive. This obsessive desire to control Alison is evident through a telling animal metaphor:

> Jalous he was, and heeld hire narwe in cage,
> For she was wylde and yong, and he was old.   (116–17)

As well as showing how much he restrained and controlled her, these lines are also ironic because it is precisely in her *cage* (line 116), i.e. his house, where she is both easily tempted and easily able to go behind his back and sleep with the scheming younger clerk.

There are further indications of his stupidity. It is unlikely that he would have known the teachings of Cato, *That bad man sholde wedde his simylitude* (line 120), but nevertheless, by mention of this, his ignorance is drawn to our attention, and even more directly we are also told that *his wit was rude* (line 119). At the end of this introductory section to John, an animal image is again used, this time about him directly:

> But sith that he was fallen in the snare,
> He moste endure, as oother folk, his care.   (123–4)

Who is actually trapped? John, or his wife?

Activity

In what ways is John ignorant and what are his strengths as a character?

Discussion

If John has to *endure... his care* (line 124), what does that suggest about him? Is he a character who lives at the mercy of other characters manipulating and controlling him? While this appears to be the case at home, where he is duped by his wife and, more significantly, by the scholarship of his clever lodger, we can derive a totally opposite impression from our view of John, the carpenter. As a craftsman he is an accomplished expert. Although we may laugh at his unwitting belief in the coming of the flood and at all the steps he has to take to save his wife, there is no doubting his professional skill as he attempts to control the situation. We also know that he is highly respected locally as a carpenter, both by implication that his unfortunately timed absence was due to a call on his trade at Osney and through what we learn about him from the lines spoken by the cloisterer to Absolon (lines 556–62).

When Nicholas begins to fool John with his elaborate and carefully worked plan, John is worried about his lodger, shut away in his room, and responds with a tone of pained anxiety, which sharply reveals his limited and gullible nature. Ironically, in view of Nicholas's main purpose with the trick, John completely and quite ridiculously trusts his cunning lodger. As well as worrying that Nicholas may die, he complains of the world as being unstable, almost as if nothing can ever again be normal: *This world is now ful tikel, sikerly.* (line 320) In an ironic way he is right that the world – his world – is *now ful tikel*, but he misunderstands how. This morbid disposition rather betrays his age – he appears like a man full of woe, out of control and with little enjoyment left in life. He stresses this with his own morbid example:

> 'I saugh today a cors yborn to chirche
> That now, on Monday last, I saugh hym wirche.' (321–2)

John is also mocked by the Miller for his pride in being ignorant: *blessed be alwey a lewed man* (line 347) and his unwise smugness is also evident as John explains (to Alison, presumably) how Nicholas's astrology has driven him mad:

> 'This man is falle, with his astromye,' (343)

Activity

During the long exchange between Nicholas and John (lines 366–502) in what ways does John reveal his gullibility?

Discussion

John is continually persuaded to take action against the unbelievable possibility of the second flood through his religious faith and simple beliefs. He has a pitifully simplistic view of obedience and damnation, and is immediately persuaded by Nicholas that he must keep the secret:

> 'Nay, Crist forbade it, for his hooly blood!'
> Quod tho this sely man, 'I am no labbe,
> Ne, thogh I seye, I nam nat life to gabbe.
> Sey what thou wolt, I shal it never telle
> To child ne wyf, by hym that harwed helle!' (400–4)

As Nicholas's well-worked practical joke unfolds, John shows not just how stupid he is – we greet with incredulity the idea of the coming of the second flood and his belief in it – but also how foolish, contradictory and wrong he has been. He is taken in by the very contentions that he has dismissed. Indeed, as he tries to make sense

This engraving of Noah building the ark was published as the title page in the *Nuremburg Chronicle* in 1493

A thirteenth-century Italian-Byzantine mosaic showing Noah freeing the animals from the ark

of Nicholas's trance, he recalls, with a kind of ignorant authority, the story of the philosopher who fell into the *marle-pit* while out walking and gazing at the stars. He says that Nicholas *shal be rated of his studiyng*. When he gains access to Nicholas's room he attempts to deliver Nicholas from his trance by simplistically incanting language and supplications, which are a cross between prayers and spells. If this stupidity and gullibility were not enough, John reveals even more how his actions contradict his beliefs when he responds to Nicholas's astrological arguments about the flood and its danger to Alison, with complete faith in what he is being told, even asking Nicholas how he might deal with the problem:

> This carpenter answerde, 'Allas, my wyf!
> And shal she drenche? Allas, myn Alisoun!'
> For sorwe of this he fil almoost adoun,
> And seyde, 'Is ther no remedie in this cas?'   (414–17)

While looking for signs of John's utter stupidity and gullibility – which present him as a pathetic character – you may like to look also at line 429, when he meekly says that he remembers the story of Noah *ful yoore ago*.

Activity

Nicholas persuades John of the coming of the flood and of the need to take ridiculous precautions against it. Explore John's reactions to the plan and show how his character is further revealed through his actions and speech as he falls for the joke.

Discussion

I find many features of John's character concentrated in the section beginning at line 503. He confirms his jealous love for Alison and shows that he will behave irrationally as a result of his devotion. These insights are delivered in an elevated style of language from the Miller, perhaps suggesting that human behaviour is controlled by powerful emotions, but also mocking John, reminding us that he has no idea what is actually happening: *Lo, which a greet thyng is affeccioun!* (line 503). Remember that he has earlier been taken in by Nicholas's religious persuasion, so much so that he believes it would be sinful to be in the company of his wife. This is the simple side to John, so simple that Nicholas knows he can see through the absurd yet elaborate plan without any trouble. Then comes a very practical side to his character: the man at work. Having got over his *sory cheere* (line 510), he sets about the task of saving his wife from the coming flood with professional skill. He fastens the *knedyng trogh* and *kymelyn* as instructed and with:

> His owene hand he made laddres thre, (516)

Does this suggest frenetic work? Getting everything ready in order to save himself and Alison?

Furthermore, he carefully provides food and drink for his confinement, and so is in a state of as much readiness for the coming disaster as he could possibly be. Chaucer confirms his practical disposition in the line: [he]... *dressed alle thyng as it sholde be.* (line 527) Is there a contradiction implied in this: is he foolish of mind yet so clever of hand? His simple, religious but superficial faith is once again brought out as he says his prayers and awaits the onset of the rain: yet any fool should know there could be no second flood!

Finally, it may occur to you that there is a reminder of his age. He falls asleep in curfew time. Is another contrast implied by this, remembering what Nicholas and Alison are doing at the same time?

The courtly characters

The other three main characters, Nicholas, Alison and Absolon, are all presented, at least for some of the time, as mock courtly characters. Chaucer gives each of them characteristics, conventions and diction borrowed from the codes of courtly love. Courtly love needs to be thought of as a kind of game in fourteenth-century life acted out using certain actions and styles of language, and its ultimate aim was inevitably sexual conquest. As has already been explained, there is a parallel in *The Miller's Tale* with the true courtly romance in *The Knight's Tale*. There, two knights were rivals in love in remote Athens; here two clerks are rivals in contemporary Oxford.

Critics have drawn their evidence for the idea of a courtly parody in the three main characters from the language. Constant use of the word *hende* as an epithet for Nicholas marks him out as a kind of hero lover and his skill at secret love (*Of deerne love he koude and of solas* [line 92]) also marks him out as skilful in the courtly codes of behaviour. The language used to describe Alison presents her as a desirable conquest, yet the idealism in the beauty of women in courtly love is mocked at the end of the description. Other writers used the phrase *In al this world...* in order to exaggerate the unsurpassable beauty of their courtly women. Chaucer uses the same hyperbole in his impressions of Alison, only to hint that she was a rather more basic woman, *wenche* having a connotation of 'slut' for the reader. In many ways the parody of a courtier in the description of Absolon surpasses that of Nicholas, although he is a lot less manly than Nicholas. Where Nicholas is *hende* (clever), Absolon is *joly* and in his joliness he energetically plays the part of a courtly lover, albeit a very unsuccessful one!

One of the ways in which Chaucer parodies courtliness in Nicholas and Alison, who really are lovers, is by reducing their behaviour to a low common denominator of sexuality.

Nicholas

Nicholas is one of the liveliest and cleverest characters in *The Canterbury Tales*. His introduction suggests a complex character and certainly somebody quite capable of outwitting the simple-minded carpenter. As well as being a scholar (a very different sort of scholar to the unworldly pilgrim described by Chaucer in the *General Prologue*), he is also given an individualizing characteristic through his hobby of astrology, which he will put to such good use in the trick he plays on John. The study of astrology was popular in Chaucer's society, but his interest in the subject may have been included for reasons that help us to understand

Nicholas's character and explain his actions. Consider carefully what we are told about his hobby:

> If that men asked hym, in certein houres
> Whan that men sholde have droghte or elles shoures,
> Or if men asked hym what sholde bifalle
> Of every thyng; I may nat rekene hem alle. (87–90)

The impression is of a character who thoroughly enjoys the calculations and speculations which are part of astrology. As we delve into Nicholas's character, what we discover is a young man who seems to enjoy scheming and planning as much as the end results of his schemes. It may have occurred to you that Nicholas could have found easier ways of having sex with Alison, so it is possible that the enjoyment of the intrigue in the trick he plays on John, using his knowledge of astrology, is almost as satisfying for him as his eventual sexual conquest. Although clearly the description of his night in bed with Alison suggests that it was very fulfilling!

The complexity of Nicholas's character is built up with some carefully selected features, all of which play their part in his behaviour during the remainder of the tale. There are three elements to his character that are expressed using similar techniques to those used by Chaucer in the descriptions of the pilgrims in the *General Prologue*: description of physical appearance; mention of possessions; followed by a catalogue of accomplishments, or skills. His room smells sweetly of herbs and he too shows that he is conscious of his own body by adorning it to make it:

> ... as sweete as is the roote
> Of lycorys or any cetewale. (98–99)

The way that his books and the equipment used for astronomy are so carefully laid out, plus what we learn about his accomplished singing and musical skills, make Nicholas seem very successful as a scholar. It is also a mockery of courtliness. Although not a courtier himself, he possesses many of the skills associated with courtly life and there are hints in the language that Chaucer means him to be compared with Arcite in *The Knight's Tale*. Nicholas is *Allone, withouten any compaignye* in his Oxford lodgings, just as Arcite was *Allone, withouten any compaignye*, although that was at the point of his death.

Activity

How is courtliness presented in the descriptions of Nicholas?

Discussion

In courtly romance, love was idealized – placed on a higher and noble plane – and it always involved rituals. Consider the way in which this sort of idealism is mocked by Nicholas's character. In some respects both his appearance as a man and his wooing of Alison are conventional in a courtly style. What can you find about his appearance? How accomplished is he as a singer and musician? Then look closely at the section when he first attempts to woo Alison (lines 163–198). What are the love rituals he goes through and how do you think they might differ from those of a real courtier? Courtiers were expected to present their longing for their chosen woman, a plea which would often be rejected, leaving them to try even harder with the skills at their disposal.

So what are we to make of the way he approaches Alison?

> And prively he caughte hire by the queynte,
> And seyde, 'Ywis, but if ich have my wille,
> For deerne love of thee, lemman, I spille'. (168–70)

(See Notes, p. 60 for an understanding of the sexual connotation in this description.)

When Alison rather lamely rejects his first advances we see more of his apparent courtliness:

> This Nicholas gan mercy for to crye,
> And spak so faire, and profred him so faste,
> That she hir love hym graunted atte laste, (180–2)

This is further mockery of courtly behaviour: he is the forlorn lover racked with pain and anguish at his rejection. As Alison accedes to his request (with great speed as it happens), Chaucer returns to the other prominent side of Nicholas's character, his love of scheming and planning, and to one of the main medieval themes of the story, the cuckolding. He tells Alison that he would be wasting his time if he were not able to deceive a carpenter.

The word *hende* is used many times to describe Nicholas, so much so that we probably need to seek irony in it. In essence it meant 'courteous' but with Nicholas it is usually assumed that his courtesy – his grace and charm (if you like, a kind of winning charm) – were all put to the tasks of seducing Alison and taking John in. *Hende* also has a connotation of being clever. How clever do you find Nicholas? As we learn, there is another side to his character, which is far from charming or courtly. His audacious sexual advance on Alison and the way he *leet fle a fart* (line 698) on the hapless Absolon give a very different impression.

Hende could also mean 'near at hand'. How might there be an irony in this meaning?

Activity

Following the introduction to Nicholas, it is his actions and most especially his speech that characterize him. What do we learn about him from his actions and from the considerable amount of speech that he is given in the tale?

Discussion

With John out of the way, Nicholas goes quickly into action, unceremoniously grabbing hold of Alison *by the queynte* (line 168), telling her that he will die for her love. Slightly rebuffed, he then becomes extremely charming: *And spak so faire, and profred him so faste*, (line 181) with the result that she gives in. We see his lust, his self-confident boldness and his courtly charm coming out in this passage, which is written in a style full of pace and energy. But what follows may be even more revealing of his character. Alison may have welcomed his advances, but she points out that, because John is such a jealous husband, Nicholas is going to have to be secretive in order to bed her. Is it at this point that Nicholas is revealed in his truest light?

> 'Nay, thereof care thee noght,' quod Nicholas.
> 'A clerk hadde litherly biset his whyle,
> But if he koude a carpenter bigyle.' (190–2)

Nicholas is going to relish the plan he will set to beguile John. Is the delight in setting the trap going to be as rewarding as the pleasure he will gain from the eventual night in bed with Alison? Many critics have observed that, because John is away at Osney, there was nothing to stop them from having sex at this point of the poem. Remember also that he had grabbed hold of her crutch and so his intentions were fairly clear. Why do they delay, especially when the plan to keep John at bay is such a complex one and when you consider that it is going to put Nicholas to some trouble to set it in motion? In line 297, we read that the plot against John is a *game*.

A feature of the plot is its sheer ingenuity. Another is the way that Nicholas knows that he is playing on John's religious fears and superstitions. Nicholas's apparent disappearance is enough to give the simple carpenter a sense that something is wrong, so he sends his servant, Robyn, up to Nicholas's room. The servant manages to look into the room through a hole in the wall (the cat's hole!). Nicholas appears to be in a trance. What strikes me is the completeness of his act: he doesn't simply pretend when necessary; it is more that he is acting all the time, having entered fully into the spirit of the deception.

> This Nicholas sat evere capyng upright,
> As he had kiked on the newe moone. (336–7)

The deceit is later compounded when Nicholas speaks with John. He combines tones of great friendliness with religious and scientific authority, plus a kind of moral blackmail, convincing the carpenter that Alison is in danger. He brings to mind the horror of the supposed flood in a vivid and frightening picture and then convinces John, really through playing on John's areas of gullibility, of what he needs to do to save himself and his wife.

We can see Nicholas's speech to John as a wonderful example of rhetorical deception. He uses so many persuasive techniques, so that the poor gullible John, foolish and simple man that he is, stands no chance of avoiding the deception. Essentially, Nicholas's argument is based on the apparent authority of his astrological predictions preying on John's faith and fears.

Do we judge Nicholas at this point? Is it fair that he should mould John's behaviour with so much manipulation?

Alison

In courtly fashion, Alison is the pretty and immensely desirable heroine, indeed unsurpassed in her beauty. See the Notes (pp. 56–9) for a reminder of how Chaucer parodies the appearance of a courtly heroine in the details he uses to describe her. Perhaps the best example of how Alison's credentials as a courtly lover are undermined and reduced is the animal simile used to describe her delightful body:

> Fair was this yonge wyf, and therwithal
> As any wezele hir body gent and smal.   (125–6)

Can you see how Chaucer is juxtaposing courtly elegance and appearance with an impression of her animal instincts, further supported by her sexual eagerness? Consider her clothing: it suggests the decorative, starched prettiness of a country maiden; her headband is worn high, showing off her forehead; her physical appearance is twice compared to fruit trees; a beautifully adorned purse hangs down by her belt. This busy country wench is positively seductive and enticing:

> There nys no man so wys that koude thenche
> So gay a popelote or swich a wenche.   (145–6)

Comparisons of a kind have been made between Alison and the portrait of the Prioress in the *General Prologue*. The description of the Prioress is generally assumed to be one of the most ironic sections of the whole poem. Chaucer cleverly describes her physical appearance, and other attributes, to hint at a supposedly religious woman who is in fact as vain and self-conscious as any courtly lady. The comparison lies in the restraint. When he describes the Prioress in the *General Prologue*, Chaucer points to aspects of her appearance that would have been expected in a courtly romantic heroine: a well-formed nose, a small mouth and wide forehead. There is restrained irony in the description; merely hinting at the way this lady from a religious order is more like a courtly heroine.

In the description of Alison, the restraint is of a different sort. Here the courtly heroine is described in detail. Chaucer runs his eyes over every part of her appearance, with details of what she wore from top to toe! These include a belt decorated with strips of silk, a white apron, embroidered collar, a wide headband to reveal her high forehead (this is similar to a feature of the Prioress) and a purse lavishly decorated with brass beads hanging from her belt. So how is this 'restraint'? It may appear quite the opposite! If you look closely at the physical appearance you will find that Chaucer is drawing attention to her beautiful young body by asking the reader to gaze on her attractiveness, much like Nicholas has done. The best example, although not the only one, is the folds of her apron:

> **A barmclooth as whit as morne milk**
> **Upon hir lendes, ful of many a goore.**　　　　　　　(128–9)

Goore meant a kind of fold, but more accurately a triangular strip of cloth. Perhaps the restraint at this point of the description is that Chaucer merely describes her clothing, when he is in fact really drawing attention to what lies beneath it. Indeed he reminds the reader, perhaps unnecessarily, of the position of her apron: *upon hir lendes*. Certainly, as the description of Alison continues, he becomes noticeably less restrained in such lines as:

> Hir shoes were laced on hir legges hye.
> She was a prymerole, a piggesnye,
> For any lord to leggen in his bedde,
> Or yet for any good yeman to wedde. (159–62)

Activity

Look carefully at lines 149–62. In these lines there are many references to animals and nature. What sort of impression do they give of Alison's character? How do her actions later in the poem justify these sorts of descriptions?

Discussion

Alison is revealed as lively and flirtatious, and she has a skittish, playful energy which is forward (in the sexual sense) and bold:

> Wynsynge she was, as is a joly colt,
> Long as a mast, and upright as a bolt. (155–6)

This energy and sexual eagerness are continued in the first main part of the action that she is involved in. When Nicholas takes hold of her and starts to make arrangements for the seduction, her reaction is to behave like a truly disdainful courtly mistress, although this is described through a clever simile that emphasizes the natural and playful behaviour she indulges in:

> And she sproong as a colt dooth in the trave,
> And with hir heed she wryed faste awey,
> And seyde, 'I wol nat kisse thee, by my fey!
> Why, lat be!' quod she. Lat be, Nicholas,
> Or I wol crie "out, harrow" and "allas"!
> Do wey youre handes, for youre courteisye!' (174–9)

The mockery lies in the fact that she so assertively rejects Nicholas's advances – this would have been part of the expected ritual of a courtly lover – only to show a line or two later that, in spite of such a melodramatic reaction, she *wol been at his comandement*. Does this change of heart surprise us?

You will have noticed how the descriptions of Alison are so vivid and natural. There is a physical side to her character, which can sometimes be seen as bordering on vulgarity. If not yet vulgar, she is certainly sensual, vain, brash and impetuous. These traits are all established through the natural and animal imagery, mostly delivered through simile: her song like the swallow's; her movements like the capering of a kid goat or calf; and her mouth as sweet as a *hooard of apples leyd in hey or heeth* (line 154). Does her poetic attachment to the natural world help to prepare us for her most important contribution to the *fabliau* plot when at the window *out she putte hir hole* (line 624)? She also finds it hilarious that Absolon should have *kiste hir naked ers* (line 626). She certainly shows no hesitation or shame in behaving in such a compromising way, and we suspect that if Nicholas had not stuck his own bum out of the window on the second occasion, *she* would have done the same again.

Absolon

It is perhaps in the character of Absolon, easily the least successful and the most psychologically harmed of the three young 'lovers', where we find the strongest mockery of courtly love. That is because he behaves most consciously like a typical courtier. The mockery becomes almost burlesque in style – a satirical imitation in a character lampooned and doomed to failure.

Some of Chaucer's language might lead us to believe that Absolon is actually a rather effeminate character and in this respect he seems to contrast directly with Nicholas. There is another link with the Prioress from the *General Prologue*, although of course we cannot be certain that it is one that Chaucer intended. Like the Prioress, Absolon has grey eyes, a trait that Chaucer otherwise reserved for female characters. Notice too that Absolon has a red complexion – probably not intended as rustic and manly, more a feminine shade – and he is also frequently described as *joly*. (See Notes, p. 63.) This word, which variously means 'lovely' or 'pretty', again marks him out as effeminate and of course contrasts with the often used *hende* applied to Nicholas.

Absolon is intensely self-conscious, to the point of affectation, and very aware of his appearance. To understand this, consider, for example, the attention he pays to his hairstyle:

> Crul was his heer, and as the gold it shoon,
> And strouted as a fanne large and brode;
> Ful streight and evene lay his joly shode. (206–8)

His proud and fanciful approach to life is confirmed in the classic Chaucerian description of his clothing. The descriptions of his shoes, hose, tunic, and gown are full of a mixture of bright and delicate colours, and elaborate designs, with fastidious care taken over the fine details of his appearance. It was unusual for a man to be described in so much physical detail; these descriptions were usually reserved for female characters.

If he *looked* the part of a courtly lover then he could also *behave* like one, or at least he tried to. He could dance, although perhaps in a rather elaborate style (*and with his legges casten to and fro*), he could play the guitar and he could sing, although the fact that he sang high treble may suggest that his voice may not have broken – presumably another attempt to undermine his sexuality.

While we remain suspicious as to how far he was successful, he was a womanizer of sorts, or at least saw himself as one. But even though he entertained all the barmaids of the town with his accomplished singing, he was saving himself for Alison, the carpenter's wife. He is described as having a *love-longynge* (line 241) for Alison. Like a truly practised and intent courtier, unable to sleep at night, he would go to her window and sing *in his voys gentil and smal* (line 252):

> 'Now deere lady, if thy wille be,
> I praye yow that ye wole rewe on me.' (253–4)

You have reflected on the descriptions of his appearance and clothing. How do you interpret the work that he did and the skill he possessed? In letting blood, he would have been performing basic and rather gruesome medical acts, although this would have placed him lower in a pecking order compared to theoretical physicians, as would his drawing up of legal contracts. Is there a suggestion that, in comparison to Nicholas, he is inferior and lacking in his rival's levels of intelligence? (See Notes, p. 62.)

It is impossible to avoid some consideration of the similarity between the name Absolon and the biblical character, Absalom. If you want to read the whole story of Absalom, you will find it in Samuel 2, Chapters 14–18. Here are a few key points about Absalom. Decide whether you think Chaucer had them in mind when he created the somewhat ridiculous character of Absolon. In all Israel everyone acknowledged that there was no man as handsome as Absalom; from the sole of his feet to the top of his head he was perfect in appearance; when he shaved his head, he used to weigh the hair at three pounds according to the king's weight; he was well known for getting up early (he would stand at the city gates in Jerusalem and question people coming into the city to see if they were loyal to the king); he led an 'insurrection' against David – a rebellion or uprising. Absalom came to a sad end. While leading his troops to war, he got his hair caught in the branches of a large oak tree and was suspended in mid-air. After hanging there for some while, he was put to death by having three spears struck into him. Perhaps another part of the story worthy of note is that Absalom had sex with his father's concubines (prostitutes) in a tent on a roof 'in the sight of all Israel'!

Of course there are no direct parallels between the story from the Book of Samuel and the story of Absolon in *The Miller's Tale*. Nevertheless, consider whether Chaucer was intending to imitate or parody the Bible. Also, try and conclude whether the biblical links add to the mockery of Absolon as a character.

Activity

Look closely at the description of Absolon's efforts to woo Alison in lines 163–76. What sort of 'courtly lover' does he try to be? What are the characteristics of his efforts to be a courtly lover and how well, or badly, does he play the role of a romantic hero?

Discussion

Unquestionably this foolish man fits into a tradition about courtly love. This was sometimes called *fine amour*. An activity which often involved the pursuit of someone else's wife, it was a series of attentions that treated women with enormous respect. It was amorous behaviour involving a sort of craft, or code, full of ritual and message designed to attract the woman. This often involved cultural and artistic accomplishments such as poetry, song and dance. The very act of offering love in this manner would be a way of ennobling the courtier (giving status), and yet the woman would be expected to reject him and make herself an even greater prize for the lover's advances. Sometimes the ritual of love games could lead to outcomes of tragic intensity, on other occasions it was simply farce.

In the passage that describes Absolon's attempts to woo Alison, consider the attention he pays her, the gifts he offers and the dramatic tone in which he speaks to her. Do you think he is capable of being seductive?

The form of the story is constructed so that the reader will be aware from the outset of the futility of Absolon's efforts. Notice that he is introduced in a long passage of the poem just after Nicholas has gained Alison's consent to have sex with him. Nicholas reveals his delight in anticipation by playing fast music and Alison, somewhat ironically in view of her sinful intentions, sets about her work in the *paryssh chirche*. So, even when Absolon is introduced, the outcome of the secret love between his rival (Nicholas) and his intended prize (Alison) has been determined. Later, Chaucer belittles his attempts to play the courtly lover with a reminder of the pointlessness of what he is doing:

> But what availleth hym as in this cas?
> She loveth so this hende Nicholas
> That Absolon may blowe the bukkes horn;
> He ne hadde for his labour but a scorn.   (277–80)

Poor Absolon becomes progressively the victim of more self-deception. By concentrating on John's absence from home, he misses the point about his real rival (Nicholas). He has not seen John stir after the foolish carpenter has shut himself away in his attic and he interprets this as an opportunity:

> This Absolon ful joly was and light,
> And thoghte, 'Now is tyme to wake al nyght,
> For sikirly I saugh hym nat stirynge
> Aboute his dore, syn day bigan to sprynge.' (563–6)

When on this occasion he goes to Alison's window, the techniques of characterization are marked. In a remarkable passage (lines 579–99), Absolon prepares himself as a lover in a manner that both parodies the courtly romantic hero – not least in his dialogue in lines 606–11 – and, frankly, reveals his physical inadequacies. The courtier is evident in the way that he dresses himself handsomely and makes himself smell so sweet. He uses endearing terms of affection and the language of popular love songs to try and arouse her feelings. (Remember all the time what she has been doing and who she is with!) The physical mockery is evident in the condition he admits he is in and the unusual choice of imagery:

> 'Wel litel thynken ye upon my wo,
> That for youre love I swete ther I go.
> No wonder is thogh that I swelte and swete;
> I moorne as dooth a lamb after the tete'. (593–6)

We also learn earlier in the poem that, as a result of his *love-longynge*, his mouth *hath icched al this longe day* (line 574).

This mixture of physical or sensual pleasure and awkwardness prepares us for what is about to happen. The true Absolon, who springs back in disgust from his unfortunate kiss, is suddenly a very different kind of character to the apparently accomplished courtly lover kneeling by Alison's window.

Now the physical attributes suggest disgust and even self-loathing. In a fit of anger he *froteth now his lippes/With dust, with sond, with straw, with clooth, with chippes* (lines 639–40) and we learn that he is cured of his longing for love.

We might have been prepared for this reversal when we learned earlier of his squeamishness, and there is an even more subtle way in which his prowess as a courtly lover is mocked. On the evening before he first goes to Alison's window, he decides to take a nap, but in fact oversleeps, hardly the sign of a true and ardent lover. There is a juxtaposition of the lines:

> 'Therfore I wol go slepe an houre or tweye,
> And al the nyght thanne wol I wake and pleye.' (577–8)

with:

> Whan that the firste cok hath crowe, anon
> Up rist this joly lovere Absolon, (579–80)

Activity

Investigate the way that Absolon takes revenge. How strong is his desire for revenge and how does he go about it?

Discussion

His quest to get hold of the *hoote kultour* (line 668) and the way he uses it is intended to do real harm to Alison and in fact leads him to take the skin off another man's buttocks. We know from the haste and secrecy with which he acquires the red-hot poker from Gerveys, the blacksmith, just how premeditated his violent intentions were. What do you make of this vicious behaviour? Is it to be interpreted merely as part of the comic plot or does it express other features of Absolon's character?

One of the roles of Gerveys, the blacksmith, is probably to contribute to the backdrop of realism that runs throughout the story, but another reason for sketching his manner as so easy-going and unvexed may be to provide a contrast with the now terse and single-minded Absolon. Indeed, are we to interpret Absolon's current intentions as more purposeful than his earlier amorous activities? In the end, he has certainly gained revenge, but does that make us sympathetic towards him as a character? I suspect not.

Language, style, and structure

In the way that he adapted *fabliau*, Chaucer introduced characters and made them vivid as people rather than simply stock types who would have existed only to fulfil the expectations of the form. As you have seen, three of the main characters are introduced by pen portraits and the fourth, John, is equally brought to life through his actions and most of all through his work. There remain elements of typical *fabliau* and the story itself is very far-fetched. Nevertheless, unlike many other tales told by the pilgrims, and most certainly in complete contrast with *The Knight's Tale*, the story abounds with realism. There may be references to biblical stories and superstitious forewarnings, and John certainly imagines the coming of the second flood, but never once does the action deviate from the everyday working life of Oxford and it actually hardly moves outside John's house. (Many of the other tales that have partially realistic settings also include elements of classicism, illusions and magic and they sometimes contain characters who seem more symbolic than realistic).

Realism

What is actually meant by the term 'realism' when we apply it to Chaucer in a work such as *The Miller's Tale*? Charles Muscatine in his essay, 'Style of the Man and Style of the Work' (see Brewer, 1966, p. 105), describes Chaucer's realism in this way:

> [the realism] asserts in various ways the primacy of matter and of animal nature in human concerns; accordingly, [it is a style] compounded of domestic imagery, natural discourse, local setting.

To us in the twenty-first century, when we try to define realism, we think of places, people and events that, good or bad, liked or disliked, we can genuinely see in our minds. We conceive of realism as something recognizable and predictable, rather than abstract or symbolic. In medieval life, it was not so much visualizing people or places as real that mattered – although we must be eternally grateful to Geoffrey Chaucer for leaving us such a window on the medieval world – but the importance of including traits of behaviour in literature that would not normally have been there. Put another way, we are surprised nowadays if literature, film or the theatre are not realistic; it is likely the surprise would have been the other way round in Chaucer's day. A realistic style tended to create a more basic and earthy interpretation of human behaviour, dealing with functions of life that were never part of rhetoric, elevated description and other more lofty styles of writing. To put the point more crudely, Chaucer was introducing his readers to the reality that all aspects of human behaviour could be the subject of literature, and not just fine emotions or noble acts of heroism. If you think about the basic life elements in *The Miller's Tale*, you will recognize that here Chaucer's characters exhibit their natural functions as well as, or perhaps more than, their moral purposes.

Activity

To understand the range of realism presented in the poem, do the following tasks which will all involve you going through and checking references in the poem.

- Survey and analyse the poem to find all the evidence you can of characters at work, conducting business, at play, performing bodily functions. (It is even worth noting how many references there are to parts of the human body!)
- List all the implements, tools and instruments that are referred to.
- Make a timeline for the activities of the characters and locate their actions in the correct settings.
- Check all the references to John's house and compare your impression of it with the reconstructed drawing on p. 134.

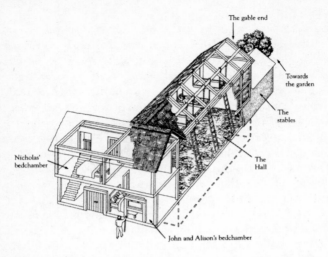

The gable end

Towards
the garden

The
stables

Nicholas'
bedchamber

The
Hall

John and Alison's bedchamber

A reconstruction of John's house based on the descriptions in *The Miller's Tale*.

This painting by Jean Bourdichon (1457–1521) shows a medieval carpenter in his workshop with the tools of his trade

Discussion

There are regular references to commonplace objects. One of the more vivid is the clear visual impression of the door that leads into Nicholas's room:

> An hole he foond, full lowe upon a bord,
> Ther as the cat was wont in for to crepe,   (332–3)

What have you noticed about the style of language used to describe them? Can you see how the everyday, matter-of-fact world forms a natural part of the language? It might strike you that the style used to refer to commonplace objects and actions is undramatic, slow, leisurely, even rather dawdling, as if there is nothing remarkable or surprising about the real world that these characters inhabit. Yet this reference to the real and familiar medieval world is sometimes set against other styles, and there is a continual contrast between the real world in which the characters go about their business and a motif that is far-fetched and absurd, the stuff of make-believe, such as the evocation of the coming of the flood.

John's long speech to Nicholas when he is outside his chamber (lines 341–59) is a rhetorical mixture of anecdote, supplication (almost like prayer), exclamation, analogy, and universal warning. Then, almost as if he returns to the need for practical decisions, he asks Robyn to break down the door:

> 'Get me a staf, that I may underspore,
> Whil that thou, Robyn, hevest up the dore.'   (357–8)

As if to underline still further the contrast between realism and absurdity, there are references to earlier sections of the poem, with the Miller appearing to play a 'cameo' part in his own story. The Miller's name, as we know from his own prologue, is Robyn, and in the *General Prologue* Chaucer introduces him as a *stout carl for the nones*. Robyn, the servant, who appears in the tale, is described similarly as a *strong carl for the nones*.

Objects from everyday life are used throughout the planning for the flood and realism mixes with irony and farce. It is such an absurd undertaking, but the planning is meticulous, performed by John with craftsmanship and professionalism, driven on by his irrational fear of the danger to his wife. After a typically dramatic passage in the poem, which vividly dramatizes his anguish (*He wepeth, weyleth, maketh sory cheere;/He siketh with ful many a sory swogh* (lines 510–11), there follows a detailed inventory of his construction and planning, including detail about the ladder he will use to climb into the loft, the food and drink he will store and the dispatch of his servant and his servant's wife to London. Throughout this passage of the poem, realism is set against implausibility and the contrasts of style are striking.

The phrase 'mixed style' has been used to summarize Chaucer's work, suggesting that he can readily move between elevated and dramatic language when the occasion demands and a more familiar everyday realism when he needs to. As you study *The Miller's Tale* try to assess how courtly, romantic, dramatic, and heroic styles of language are positioned alongside the detailed realism. This should help you to understand the element of parody.

There are numerous other uses of realism in the tale, Chaucer using a great deal of descriptive intensity in his own development of the *fabliau*. Much of the action reflects the everyday events in the lives of the characters. John goes away for a day to Oseneye (line 166); Absolon works as a *parissh clerk* (line 204) at the *paryssh chirche* (line 199), where he set his eyes on Alison. Reference has already been made to the visit that Absolon makes to Gerveys, the blacksmith. How does this encounter contribute to the tale's sense of reality? It is also worth considering time locations. These contribute to the setting. Nicholas's and Alison's relationship starts at a particular point in time, one day

Whil that hir housbonde was at Oseneye   (166)

But they agree to wait for their adultery to take place. Nicholas begins his deception on a particular day, a Saturday, and stays in his room all weekend. Nicholas and Alison make love to the sound of the *belle of laudes*. We learn very specifically about the events of the Monday: how John willingly shuts himself away;

how Nicholas and Alison spend the night making love; and how Absolon is deceived by the chance meeting with a cloisterer at the abbey. The natural rhythms of time become very prominent at the climax of the tale: Absolon goes to Alison's window *whan that the firste cok hath crowe*; Gerveys wonders what it is that has forced Absolon to rise so early; Nicholas *was risen for to pisse*. Ironically and with obvious farce, John is woken from his slumber in the ensuing commotion and assumes that the flood has arrived.

Another kind of realism in the description of action lies in the 'raciness' of some of the behaviour. Some critics have suggested that there are features of the poem that go beyond mere 'realism'. There is a crudity to some of the actions, which of course adds to the comic effect. Other terms that have been used to describe some of the gross realism are 'naturalism' or 'animalism'. For example, while John is away in Osney, back at his house Nicholas wastes no time grabbing hold of Alison *by the queynte*. As she writhes away from him he holds her *by the haunchebones* and at the end of the encounter, he *thakked hire aboute the lendes weel*. We learn that Absolon was *somdeel squaymous/Of fartyng, and of speche daungerous*. The Miller introduces this part of Absolon's character as a part of the structure of the joke that will be played on him later, although his phobia will rebound on him in a most unlikely and unpredictable way!

In many ways these more crude aspects of the style reflect the fact that the story is about sex as much as they reflect the character of the Miller, just as many other tales appear to belong to their teller. The elements of sex in the story are unashamedly coarse and ribald, which comes as no surprise. The Miller himself has already been presented as a man of animal traits. Look back at the portrait of him in the extract from the *General Prologue* on p. 9. The imagery used to describe his beard and the colour of the hair sticking out from the wart on his nose picture him as a fox and a sow! We learn that the stories he told were mostly of *synne and harlotries* (*General Prologue*, line 561).

Perhaps the descriptions of his uncontrolled brawn, and indeed his drunkenness, add to our impression of him as a character who behaves as much like a beast as a man.

The natural and physical behaviour associated with Alison and Nicholas – Alison's attractively described body, their hasty and erotic encounters, and their prized night in bed together – need to be contrasted with the animal imagery and gross realism linked with Absolon. He is on the receiving end of the crude practical joke involving Alison's bottom and Nicholas's fart. But elsewhere an excessive physical style is used to mock him and undermine his courtly pretensions. As he contemplates going to woo Alison, he thinks:

> 'To Alison now wol I tellen al
> My love-longynge, for yet I shal nat mysse
> That at the leeste way I shal hire kisse.
> Som maner confort shal I have, parfay.
> My mouth hath icched al this longe day;
> That is a signe of kissing atte leeste.
> Al nyghte me mette eek I was at a feeste.' (570–6)

There is potentially also irony in the reference to a feast. He dreams of a feast, yet Alison and Nicholas have been at a feast of sorts in their night of pleasure. (The aim and end of fourteenth-century courtly love was a feast of sexual consummation).

The physical features used to describe Absolon's love-longing and despairing attraction for Alison anticipate the discomfort that he will eventually suffer, and the animal imagery used to present him is degrading. Perhaps the most vivid of these images is the way that he suffers (mourns) *as dooth a lamb after the tete* or that like a turtle dove he eats *na moore than a mayde*. But even earlier in the poem there is an awkward and violent image used to evoke his desire for Alison:

> I dar wel seyn, if she hadde been a mous,
> And he a cat, he wolde hire hente anon. (238–9)

This awkward physical discomfort is fully emphasized just before the infamous kiss. As he is preparing for what he thinks will be a real kiss, he rather anxiously wipes *his mouth ful drie* – hardly the actions of a desirable or manly courtier.

At this point of the poem, the Miller holds back nothing in the extreme realism of his style. We are told the full details of what Abslon does as he is forced to bring his (dry) mouth into contact with Alison's pubic hair, which, it may not have escaped your attention, he will have approached from behind! *He felte a thyng al rough and long yherd* (line 630). The next scene at the window is even more coarse – a climax of basic and vulgar language. Nicholas rises *for to pisse* (line 690); he wants to add to the crude fun by getting Absolon to *kisse his ers er that he scape* (line 692); there is then an extremely vivid description of his backside hanging out of the window; and all of this reaches a comic climax with the lines which recall, to the alert listener, Absolon's earlier mentioned phobia:

> **This Nicholas anon leet fle a fart**
> **As greet as it had been a thonder-dent.** (698–9)

The physical nature of the tale continues as the *hoote kultour* (line 704) is brandished by Absolon to burn the skin off Nicholas's rump.

Parody

Closely associated with realism is parody. As you have seen, the Miller attempts to express how characters ultimately live their lives in a very basic and unromantic way – as a point of ironic contrast to the courtly characters in *The Knight's Tale*. Thus realism is one way of undermining heroism and courtliness. A common theme for main characters in *fabliaux* is the idea of suffering for misjudged idealism. Absolon spends much of the poem living in an illusory world and like characters in other *fabliaux*, he is made to suffer for his illusions and, as one critic has written: is 'brought back to a proper recognition of the law of nature' (see Pearsall, 'Comic Tales and Fables' in Unwin, 1985, p.167). It is as if human beings are pulled in two different directions: one towards a higher level, perhaps spiritual, romantic, heroic; the other associated with basic appetites and survival. This is reflected in the mixture of styles in *The Miller's Tale*: the familiarity of events and the down-to-earth behaviour of the characters at certain points in the tale contrast with other styles of writing, which will now be explored. This mixture contributes to a magnificent parody.

Parody is imitation. Chaucer uses features of the form and style of courtly love poetry. Even though the Miller's chosen story is vulgar and outrageous, and down to earth in the extreme, it is also a story about pretensions to courtly love and there are features of the language that imitate the style of a more courtly and heroic romantic poem.

There is recurring reference to music and other courtly pastimes. Nicholas played on his *gay sautrie* (line 105), so well that *all the chambre rong* (line 107). He also sang *Angelus ad virginem* and *the Kynges Noote* in an accomplished voice. Absolon tries to exhibit the same quality of courtly behaviour with his playing and singing. He sings to Alison beneath her window, accompanied by the playing of his gittern. A few lines later we are given an ironically attractive impression of his singing through an image: *He syngeth, brokkynge as a nyghtyngale* (line 269). Perhaps the strongest mockery of courtliness is expressed in the lines that describe Absolon as a stereotype of the vain courtier (lines 212–28). These lines should help you build up a picture of the expected behaviour of the courtier. What impression of courtly behaviour do you receive from this description? (See also in the Notes, pp. 56–9 on how the description of Alison parodies the courtly heroine.)

Moving from character to action, E.T. Donaldson in his essay, 'Idiom of Popular Poetry in *The Miller's Tale*' (Downer, 1951) suggests that Chaucer parodies closely the structure and direction of a courtly love story. The wooing would be motivated by a *love-longynge* (line 241), which Absolon suffers. There is also secret wooing and the motif of rejection by the desired woman. Another feature of medieval courtly romance would have been a feast. This could either be a literal feast – a meal – or a metaphorical feast of love. During the adultery passage of the poem, there are a number of phrases, which, it has been suggested, mock the melody and harmony that is often part of the feast idea in medieval romances. While John moans, groans and snores loudly in his sleep, Nicholas and Alison descend the ladder and *Ther was the revel and the melodye* (line 544).

Another kind of parody is to be found in religion and it is closely linked with the tale's sexual themes. Nicholas uses an elaborate prediction based on biblical reference and John's simple beliefs to arrange his night of sex with Alison. We are first introduced to the tale's religious themes when we hear about Nicholas's singing. See in the Notes (p. 54) the reference to his singing of *Angelus ad virginem* (line 108). Do we gain the impression that he sings in a state of religious devotion? Just how *blessed was his myrie throte*? Alison swears *by Seint Thomas of Kent*, granting Nicholas her love, thus agreeing to adultery in the same breath as she recalls the whole purpose of the pilgrimage that lies at the heart of *The Canterbury Tales*. We know that Alison, soon after she has agreed to satisfy Nicholas's desires, goes about doing *Cristes owene werkes* (line 200).

Activity

How is religious parody developed during the central section of the tale when Nicholas persuades John of the second coming of the flood?

Discussion

Notice how religion is never far from the centre of the tale; there are many references to Christianity and appeals to various saints. It is also worth considering the structure of the tale and how it is dependent on the false belief about the second coming of the flood. Through his hobby, Nicholas gives the impression of apparently being capable of astrological predictions and John, in spite of his religious faith, believes what Nicholas says.

When Nicholas starts his trickery, John twice swears by St Thomas (whose shrine it is that the pilgrims are travelling to in Canterbury). He also calls upon the help of St Frideswide, the local patroness of the city of Oxford. Indeed John's language is peppered with prayers to try and summon help for his afflicted lodger. This reaches a climax in the section from line 370, just before Nicholas starts to speak. John is a man of simple piety; he certainly has a strong faith, but it also makes him very gullible:

> 'What seystow?
> What! Thynk on God, as we doon, men that swynke.' (382–3)

Nicholas builds his plan and deception of John entirely around religious faith, assuring John from the outset that *it is Cristes conseil that I seye* (line 396). Nicholas continues to convince John through religious persuasion, taking considerable liberties with the faith in a way that could even be described as blasphemous. (Refer to the Notes on line 400). John is, of course, immediately taken in by the astrological prediction of the coming of the flood (*That half so greet was nevere Noes flood* (line 410)) and further by what Nicholas suggests, which was to do as *seith Salomon* to follow advice and save his wife in the same way as Noah did. Throughout this 'duping' one reason why Nicholas is so convincing is because his advice is commanding and the reason it is commanding is because it carries religious authority, with the young scholar talking to the carpenter almost like a priest would to a parishioner in need of help. (See the Notes on lines 430–5 for an understanding of the way he twists the biblical story of Noah, preferring to cite on occasions elements that come from medieval Mystery Plays rather than the Bible.) In the end he convinces John that the reason for sending away the servants is a secret of God's and that he will exist in a state of grace if he sleeps apart from his wife on the night of the flood. Notice also Nicholas's religious tone as he reaches the end of his advice. He advises John:

> That noon of us ne speke nat a word,
> Ne clepe, ne crie, but be in his preyere
> For it is Goddes owene heeste deere.   (478–80)

See also the references Nicholas makes to God's wishes in lines **484** and **487**.

Finally, the religious parody reaches blasphemous proportions when John has climbed alone into the loft, saying his prayers, while Nicholas and Alison prepare for their night of sin. Note the speed and pace of the short section that describes their love-making. One final mocking moment is the reminder that they were *In bisynesse of myrthe and of solas* at the time that bells of lauds were summoning people to church before dawn. Here the sound of the bells of religious faith, supposedly sombre in tone, seem to contribute more to the indulgent and blissful state being enjoyed by the adulterers.

Nicholas's choice of subject for the hoax, the coming of a second flood, also parodies a popular theme for medieval Mystery Plays, which were meant righteously to instruct the people. The religious allusions give rise to the idea that the tale may, perversely, contain a strong Christian message. It could be seen as a paradigm (a sort of model example) for the punishment of a trilogy of sins: lechery (Nicholas), avarice (John) and pride (Absolon). In the end you have to weigh up in your mind whether you feel that such judgements are strongly asserted or whether the element of comic farce surrounding the religion makes them less likely.

Proverbs

Reference has already been made to the mixed style of the poem, frequently a mixture of serious and elevated language alongside a more conversational tone, interspersed with some very basic and crude language. One of the themes about to be considered in the following section is that of destiny and a stylistic feature closely linked to this theme is the Miller's use of proverbs. On occasions he is given by Chaucer the opportunity to philosophize about life's affairs, either with a proverb or with an image which comes across like a proverbial saying. It is easy to pass over such moments in the tale almost without noticing them as they seem so conversational and unexceptional. The tone of these sayings and images fits well into the realistic delivery of the narrative, almost as if the Miller were chatting directly to his audience. Another term for proverbs is a 'saying' – recognizable truths which appear to be undisputed wisdom, therefore linking with destiny and fortune.

Activity

Identify and list some examples of the proverbial language in the tale. Make a note of what they mean – in these instances it is worth translating the Middle English into modern prose. Why and how are they appropriate at each of these points of the poem?

Discussion

Here are two examples, the first spoken by the Miller about Absolon's plight: in effect condemning Absolon to failure as a suitor to Alison:

> Ful sooth is this proverbe, it is no lye,
> Men seyn right thus: 'Alwey the nye slye
> Maketh the ferre leeve to be looth.'   (283–5)

The second helps to emphasize the thoughts that Absolon keeps to himself when he visits Gerveys, the blacksmith, to acquire the poker:

> He hadde moore tow on his distaf
> Than Gerveys knew,   (666–7)

Imagery

The style of imagery varies according to the character for whom it is used. Some of it contributes to the earthy quality of the tale, some of it to the courtly parody. Like the proverbial sayings, much of the imagery, both simile and metaphor, sounds conversational and it is always worth 'listening' to the tone used by each speaker as much as to the poetic quality of the imagery itself. (This is actually true of all the dialogue, not just the imagery.) The result is often considerable realism or parody. Much of the imagery is drawn from wide and varied aspects of life. Yet such versatility is not simply a display of Chaucer's knowledge, which appears to have been encyclopedic on medieval life: it is perhaps also achieving something more profound. The versatility and contrasts are like a concentration of life forces that merge into one story. There is an abundance of natural imagery, particularly associated with Alison, drawn from hedgerow, farmyard and the animal world; on other occasions a representation of the reality of human life; and at other times images intended to mock the foolish courtly and amorous aspirations of the characters.

Activity

Consider some of the varied images used in the tale. Which areas of life and experience are represented?

Discussion

As you assess the impact of the imagery in the poem, you may notice the effect it has on bringing to life the four main characters and a lot of it is surprising and even shocking, yet as part of the overall tone of the poem, it is frequently presented in undertones.

What do you learn of Nicholas being *lyk a mayden meke for to see*? Of John who has *fallen in the snare*? Or of Alison who was:

> ... ful moore blisful on to see
> Than is the newe pere-jonette tree,
> And softer than the wolle is of a wether.   (139–41)

Can you see how natural imagery is used to characterize the main protagonists? Nicholas's submissive innocence (contained in the word *meke*) is ironic, emphasizing, on the contrary, his slyness. A truer impression of him is given of his attractiveness in the simile that soon follows:

> And he himself as sweete as is the roote
> Of lycorys or any cetewale.   (98–9)

You may still find that the sibilance in these lines also tells us something of his scheming nature.

The natural image used to describe Absolon's hair seems very appropriate for such a self-conscious and flamboyant man:

> Crul was his heer, and as the gold it shoon,
> And strouted as a fanne large and brode;   (206–7)

What is the other animal image used to indicate an aspect of Absolon? And how do you picture him through the image applied to the description of his *gay surplys* – his bright white robe?

Much of the imagery is simile rather than metaphor. This is in keeping with the narrative and proverbial tone that Chaucer so realistically lends the Miller. While a lot of these similes are drawn from the natural and animal world associated with the Miller's experience of life (remember he himself was described as a sow and a fox), there are lines where the imagery hints at a darker and more tragic side of life. As Absolon goes up to the window for the 'misdirected kiss', we learn that

> Derk was the nyght as pich, or as the cole,   (623)

(Although of course one very stunning effect of this simile is that it allows for such a stunning rhyme!)

By far the saddest image is contained in the words used to reflect Absolon's plight after he *hadde kist hir ers* (line 647). Cured of his *love-longynge* (line 241), he is destined to: *weep as dooth a child that is ybete* (line 651). Does this contrast with the earlier imagery used to describe him?

Consider also the two extended metaphors used by the Reeve in his prologue, which are commentaries on the Miller's story:

> 'But if I fare as dooth an open-ers –
> That ilke fruyt is ever lenger the wers,
> Til it be roten in mullok or in stree.'   (763–5)

'For sikerly, whan I was bore, anon
Deeth drough the tappe of lyf and leet it gon,
And ever sithe hath so the tappe yronne
Til that almoost al empty is the tonne.'   (783–6)

Do you find a bleakness and pathos in these images and if so, does
that contrast with the comic intensity of the tale that has just been
heard?

As for the preponderance of simile over metaphor, this was not
uncharacteristic of Chaucer's style. Think about the effect. Similes are
by their nature longer, perhaps allowing the realistic tone of the
storyteller to be maintained. They also allow the narrator's voice a
prominence in the tale and in a sense similes are more explanatory
than metaphors and perhaps even less 'poetic'.

The narrator's voice

The realistic tone of the narrator's voice happens in other ways
as well as through the use of imagery. The Miller is continually
interrupting his own story to help him pace it and move it
steadily along, for example:

Now, sire, and eft, sire, so bifel the cas   (163)

As clerkes ben ful subtile and ful queynte;   (167)

Now ber thee wel, thou hende Nicholas,   (289)

Look also at the final paragraph of the tale, noticing how the
Miller provides a kind of summary on the outcomes for the
characters.

Can we interpret the Miller's involvement in different ways?
Are we simply to see the technique as part of the structure of
good storytelling, keeping up the pace and maintaining interest in
and contact with the listeners (remember at the simplest level of
the form, he was retelling this tale directly to the pilgrims on the
journey). Or is the implication that he is applying a set of values

to his own story? This question might bring you to consider the question: is *The Miller's Tale* a story of moral truths or a bawdy farce? Can it be both? What does *The Reeve's Prologue* offer to a consideration of this question?

Structure

Chaucer's sense of structure in the story is acute. What you will find is that there are a number of moments, incidents and references, which, on close analysis, relate to each other. The more you look for associations and connections between one part of the story and another, the more possibilities you can find. Some of these connections are explicit, adding to the anticipation enjoyed in a work of farce. The first few lines of the tale raise the likelihood of astrology playing a key part in the plot, but perhaps the reader is not prepared for the degree of its involvement! The way that John is introduced first and foremost as a jealous older husband establishes the cuckolding theme at the centre of the tale and the early flirtatious liaison between Nicholas and Alison is a forerunner of their night

In bisynesse of myrthe and of solas, (546)

In Absolon's case, look at the number, frequency and timing of references to his mouth and what he does with it.

These are associations that spell out the element of farce. In the way he tells the story, Chaucer, or the Miller, encourages the pilgrims to anticipate connections between an attribute of each character and the subsequent comic actions. But there are also some more subtle associations, which might lead to deeper consideration of the meanings and ideas in the tale. As well as the complex religious links that have been discussed in the section on parody, there are many associations with the medieval world of work, and if you think about it, work plays a considerable role in the structure, development and comic outcome of the story.

Activity

What part does work play in the tale and what connections does work have with other ideas, themes and meanings?

Discussion

Ironically, carpenters in medieval England were frequently the ones who put on the Mystery Play of Noah's Ark. Far from presenting a Mystery Play, it is John, through his work, who is caught up in the intrigue of a kind of story. It is presumably his trade that takes him away from home in the first place, leaving Alison at the mercy of Nicholas's advances. Once he has set his plan in motion, Nicholas senses that a good way to appeal to John and make him even more gullible is to get him to associate work with hope: after being told about the coming flood, John asks rather ruefully: '*Is ther no remedie in this cas?*' (line 417), and Nicholas answers: '*If thou wolt werken after loore and reed.*' (line 419) and goes on to quote Solomon about the saving of Noah. Ironically, in the hanging of the *knedyng trogh*, the *tubbe* and the *kymelyn* John uses all his skills as a workman to contribute to his own humiliation. You may well find that John appears, through the language, as a very busy man.

By contrast, both Nicholas and Absolon, in their styles of speech and in the descriptions of how they spend their time, are characters with very little of any importance to do in life, except apparently devise clever schemes and play courtly love games. In the end, the world of work has a powerful role to play, overcoming the indolent and indulgent lives of the three courtly characters. The final and unwitting influence on events comes from the blacksmith, Gerveys. This affable chap hands over the iron blade to Absolon, rather tactfully avoiding any questions about its intended use. What may strike you about the words, manner and actions of Gerveys, the blacksmith, is his sheer ordinariness: there he is, inevitably up early for work, part of the everyday rhythm and pattern of the local world. His role is essentially a realistic and natural one in a set of absurd and farcical events. His contribution is among the most down to earth and practical in the entire tale.

Themes

Destiny, justice, and providence

Perhaps with the exception of Alison, none of the main characters concludes the tale in a situation they would have wished upon themselves at the start of the events, although, because this is comedy, the recriminations are not too severe at the end. Alison is the exception because she has enjoyed her night of passion with Nicholas, has rebuffed the irritating courtship of Absolon and her marriage, as far as we are led to believe, remains intact. But even she could not have anticipated how events would have unfolded and it was perhaps chance that took Nicholas's buttocks to the casement rather than hers on the second occasion of Absolon's visit, saving her from the indignation and pain that he had in mind. It could even be argued that Alison is contemptuously denied a punishment, as if to emphasize her sinfulness.

But what of the others? Has John been foolish to marry a wife much younger than himself and, given his jealous nature, is it just that he should be so severely cuckolded? Does Nicholas's arrogance and cleverness – remember that he was a clerk of some considerable intelligence – merit being ridiculed so painfully? And should Absolon's squeamish foppery lead to his being such a failure as a courtier and lover? In thinking about these questions, it may occur to you that the punishments for each character – if punishments they are – are extreme. Are they appropriate?

Human destiny, by its nature a very wide and grand theme, is important in many of the tales. Chaucer was interested in looking at ways in which the motivations and dispositions of individuals could affect the world, and how fate and chance events could play a part in determining the lives and futures of his characters.

In the structure and tone of *The Miller's Tale*, there is evidence early on that destiny will be a key theme. In the description of the main characters, there are a number of tensions and contradictions that set up a kind of argument that will need to be resolved in the plot. The most prominent of these tensions is clearly the mismatch in the marriage:

> **For she was wylde and yong, and he was old** (117)

As if to reinforce this discord, we soon learn, in an image that suggests Alison's irrepressible sexuality:

> **Fair was this yonge wyf, and therwithal**
> **As any wezele hir body gent and smal.** (125–6)

As a result of the full and complex description of Nicholas's bumptious character, it is difficult not to think that he needs to be cut down to size – to be taken down a peg or two! Chaucer carefully places the description of the *hende* Nicholas alongside the animalistic and rather lusty portrait of Alison, when we already know that her husband is likely to be made a *cokewold* (lines 118). The destinies of Nicholas and Alison are linked, and John's destiny is determined by their behaviour. There is no natural connection between Absolon and Nicholas. Absolon is introduced into the story as an extra character and he knows nothing about Nicholas's role. They become very closely linked, without once meeting, although clearly Alison tells Nicholas who Absolon is.

Essentially through the device of describing Alison's visits to the parish church on a holy day, Chaucer introduces Absolon:

> **Now was ther of that chirche a parissh clerk,**
> **The which that was ycleped Absolon.** (204–5)

Absolon's *love-longynge* takes him to the hinged-window on John's wall, there to plead with Alison to take mercy on his desires for her. In mock courtly fashion, he is seeking adulterous love, but all the while his assumption is that this will be at the expense of Alison's husband, John, and the real love plot that is taking place is concealed from him. Ironically, John is stirred to express minor irritation at Absolon's activities:

> 'What! Alison! Herestow nat Absolon,
> That chaunteth thus under oure boures wal?'   (258–9)

What we have is a series of incidents involving the characters that take place in ignorance of what others are up to. They are all destined towards a dramatic (and in Nicholas's case, a painful) climax as a result of their characteristics and behaviour. The creator of these destinies is the storyteller (Chaucer through his Miller). He hints throughout at the illusions suffered by the characters, and at their shortcomings, which will lead them each to their destinies. Foolish as he makes others appear, Nicholas may himself be the biggest fool: however good he pretends to be at predicting the future for others, he fails to predict his own outcome. John thinks that his wife is *caged*; Absolon holds a ridiculous perception of himself as a suitor. All the while the strongest character traits of each of these three characters are too strong to allow them to see where they are going wrong.

In addition to the way that the tricks, deceits and illusions of the characters contribute to the theme of destiny, there are other features of the story that suggest that theme. Nicholas is introduced as a man who could calculate futures. When John first feels concern at Nicholas's apparent trance, he broods on the sight of a corpse, stressing, without meaning to, the frailty of human life:

> This world is now ful tikel, sikerly.
> I saugh today a cors yborn to chirche
> That now, on Monday last, I saw hym wirche.   (320–2)

(See the Note on line 372, about the way that John uses a night-charm to drive away any witchcraft that he might blame for Nicholas's apparent state.) The parody of the world's destruction through the coming of the second flood is at the centre of the poem. There are frequent references to saints and philosophers, thinkers and writers, such as St Thomas a Becket, St Paul, Cato and Ptolemy.

Think also about the proverbial style, which has already been discussed. Proverbs are about universal truths. Is it possible to interpret them as part of the underlying theme of destiny, raising questions and ideas about the fates of characters and stressing the role that knowledge, learning and ignorance play in the conduct of everyday affairs? There is possibly a contrast between the wise words of fate and destiny on the one hand, and the stupidity of human behaviour on the other.

Activity

Consider the climax of events. Is the suffering experienced by John, Nicholas and Absolon a just punishment in each case and is Alison let off lightly?

Discussion

A strong feature of the tale is its farce, and our appreciation is simply through laughter. But there is another side to it and this is the way that the characters exhibit weaknesses and shortcomings that deserve mocking. A further point is to consider whether they are each being judged.

John's deserts are simple. However we may look upon him, he appears stupid. His foolish marriage has led him to become jealous of his younger wife and, although he is conscious of the fact that he could be cuckolded, he does nothing to prevent it happening. Indeed, his concern for Nicholas exacerbates the problem for himself. He reveals that he is so obsessed with Alison, through his silly response to the idea of a flood:

> This carpenter answered, 'Allas, my wyf!
> And shal she drenche? Allas, myn Alisoun!'
> For sorwe of this he fil almoost adoun,
> And seyde, 'Is ther no remedie in this cas?'   (414–7)

153

The elaborate design of Nicholas's plan completely deceives John: the more absurd it becomes, the more he believes it and so he moans pitifully about the impending disaster. The Miller sums up his stupidity with the words:

> Men may dyen of ymaginacioun,
> So depe may impressioun be take. (504–5)

This follows John's earlier superstitions. He displays a complete lack of reason or understanding and Nicholas plays on his gullibility throughout the trick.

The extent of John's folly is further emphasized by the reaction of the local people:

> The folk gan laughen at his fantasye;
> Into the roof they kiken and they cape,
> And turned al his harm unto a jape. (732–4)

As for Nicholas, perhaps the issue of justice connects not so much with what he does, but how he does it. He is so obviously cleverer than John and he is attractive to Alison. Because he could so easily have had his way with Alison quite early in the poem, I think we might wish to judge him more for his elaborate plan than for the seduction. Although sex plays a part in the poem, the plot is actually sustained more by the plan to deceive John. Everything Nicholas does – his rhetorical language, his simulation of madness and the moral pressure he exerts on John – all combine to become an elaborate joke.

A case could be made for which is the most severe of each of the three physical punishments. Falling from the rafters of his own house, John breaks his arm; in the misdirected kiss, Absolon faces complete physical humiliation from which he will apparently never recover. If you think about it, however, Nicholas's fate – to have the skin removed from his bottom – is the most painful at the time. We probably wince more at the thought of his discomfort than we do at Absolon's and John's. What is he being punished for? Is it, conventionally, for lechery? Or has he proved himself to be just as stupid as John and Absolon? Was there a degree of over-confidence in his approach to life, which may have blinded him to his own fate?

If there is justice for Absolon's faults, it may not be for his foolishness: there are some hints at deeper weaknesses in his personality over and above his mocked attempts at courtly behaviour. Are there doubts about his sexual ability? Is he prone to self-deception? Many clues to Absolon's poor self-understanding come through Chaucer's physical descriptions. Notice in particular his hair, his complexion, the pitch of his voice, his striking phobia, the way he sweetens his breath. Perhaps the most revealing indication is the dryness of his lips as he approaches his kiss with Alison, suggesting a sexual nervousness that has been carefully covered up by his courtly rhetoric and gracious behaviour at her window.

The 'misplaced kiss', as it is sometimes rather politely referred to, is described entirely from Absolon's point of view and is handled in a deliberately mocking, simplistic tone to infer his naivety. Forced to kiss *hir naked ers* (line 626), he backs away:

> ... and thoughte it was amys,
> For wel he wiste a woman hath no berd.
> He felte a thyng al rough and long yherd,
> And seyde, 'Fy!, allas! What have I do?'   (628–31)

What does he do to his lips following this humiliation? How does his determined reaction compare with the *love-longynge* (line 241) that he felt the night before? It is interesting that there is earlier a pair of lines that can be contrasted with his wiping away the kiss from his lips:

> 'My mouth hath icched al this longe day;
> That is a signe of kissyng atte leeste.'   (574–5)

Do you find that, in spite of the obvious comedy of the situation, his destiny is almost tragic when we learn that he had been cured of love forever and, in certainly the most poignant of all the poem's images, he weeps *as dooth a child that is ybete.* (line 651)

Finally, consider again the fact that no judgement appears to have been passed on Alison. What view are we therefore to hold of her? It is unlikely we would want to blame her for sleeping with Nicholas, but surely she is partly to blame for the elaborate plot that Nicholas sets up and certainly for the treatment and degradation of Absolon. Is the absence of judgement a form of silent contempt for her outrageous behaviour or should we accept, in a light-hearted way, that what she has done is an exhibition of natural desires and really not too serious, a kind of fulfillment or providence for such a beautiful young woman?

Concealment, secrecy, and deception

Much of the tale deals with actions and attitudes attributed to characters that are kept secret from others. The theme of secrecy, or privacy, first surfaces at the start of the tale in the account of Nicholas's interest in the art of astrology. He could determine the futures and fates of people through the clever use of his scientific calculations. This lends him a mystique, a sort of incontestable expertise, which he will use to such effect in the hoaxing of John later in the poem. As well as hearing about his mysterious hobby, we also know that *he was sleigh and ful privee* (line 93).

John, on the other hand, is partly sceptical of Nicholas's apparent depth of obscure knowledge, but he lacks the sense to question the reliability of astrological prediction and, if anything, his scepticism reinforces his faith in Nicholas.

There is a marked contrast between the two characters: whereas Nicholas's plans are complex and secret, part of John's gullibility arises from his tendency to be so open about everything. He admits that he is likely to be made a cuckold due to the problems of the age gap in his marriage. He shows genuine concern for Nicholas's state of health. He complies with all the suggestions to save himself and his wife from the impending flood. One of the main reasons for the success of the hoax is that Nicholas speaks to John in such an alluring way. Interestingly, Nicholas uses the word *pryvetee* (line 385) as he entices John to listen to his warnings. This takes John into his confidence:

> This Nicholas answerde, 'Fecche me drynke,
> And after wol I speke in pryvetee
> Of certeyn thyng that toucheth me and thee.'   (384–6)

John does not know any better than to believe Nicholas's ingenious calculations and he finds the predictions all the more convincing for the confidentiality and apparent trusting tone of Nicholas's words:

> 'Now John,' quod Nicholas, 'I wol nat lye;
> I have yfounde in myn astrologye,
> As I have looked in the moone bright,
> That now...'
>
> (405–8)

Concealment is added to concealment in Nicholas's persuasive hoax and John becomes deliberately secretive himself. Convinced of the arrival of the flood and the need to keep quiet about it, he will not even tell Robyn or his maid, Gill. In the end it is John who behaves with the greater conviction that the whole affair needs to be handled secretively:

> And on the Monday, whan it drow to nyght,
> He shette his dore withoute candel-lyght,
> And dressed alle thyng as it sholde be.
>
> (525–7)

Absolon's attempts at secret seduction allow the theme to become intertwined among all four main characters. His plan is to go to John's house *at cokkes crowe* (line 567) and *Ful pryvely knokken at his wyndowe* (line 568). Absolon's attempts at concealment are different to those used by Nicholas. Both are clerks involved in seduction, but what comes across in the account of Absolon's efforts is the stupidity of his behaviour. A point of irony in the structure of the story is that he actually has no need to deceive John: John has already been deceived!

Activity

Does Absolon deceive himself? Does this explain his act of vicious revenge?

Discussion

There are some quite important points to think about concerning Absolon's attempts at deception. There is evidence, already cited, to suggest that he was neither physically nor sexually as confident as he may himself have thought. In an elaborately wrought part of the plot, he disturbs the adultery of Nicholas and Alison, although the truth of what is happening is as concealed from him as it is from John. Like John, he is wrong about everything: he is not going to be a successful lover or courtier; his 'prize' (Alison) is already committing adultery – and Absolon knows nothing about Nicholas; all his physical longings *will* be rewarded, but not by love, instead by kissing Alison's bottom and discovering the full force of John's farting!

Is it any wonder that the kiss is followed by such a vicious and secretive plan to take revenge? In the short scene with Gerveys, the blacksmith, how does Absolon's tone of speech exaggerate his secretive behaviour?

The real Absolon, as it were, is perhaps revealed through this bitter plan of action and this makes me think that he has lacked self-understanding earlier. What he does with the iron blade is the only thing he actually achieves in the whole poem. Earlier, all he has done is planned or dreamed. His secret dealings with Gerveys and his approach to Alison when he returns to her window present a sense of indignation and an attempt to restore his pride. In the end, he comes across as a man full of complex secrets, contradicting his apparent earlier confidence when he tries to play the part of the courtly lover.

Other possible themes

Because of the structure of the tale, its elements of parody and the extremes of behaviour, there are other contrasting themes, many of which have been touched upon. Consider these contrasts: youth and age; work and pleasure; learning and ignorance; moral principle and free will.

You may conclude that the tale is really about contrasting aspects of life. In *The Miller's Prologue*, during the discussion about the merits of the Knight's tale and the need for a moral equivalent to follow it, themes and standards of moral and spiritual correctness are established. Throughout the tale itself, morality, either as it is being mocked or in John's faith, is never far from the reader's attention. But as you will see in the Critical Views section of this book, an alternative view of life is the one that is perhaps revealed as stronger. If the Knight's truth about life was one of high moral principle, the Miller gives voice to other principles that seem equally important: to freedom of will; to basic instincts; to the real world in which people would wish to satisfy their human desires. Can you relate these kinds of contrasts to the actions of the characters?

Critical views

Critics have examined *The Miller's Tale* from a variety of viewpoints in order to look at different meanings it might contain. Here are some of the approaches they have taken.

Origins and derivations of the *fabliau* and Chaucer's use of the form

Many critics have written at length about the way that Chaucer used the form of *fabliau*. *Fabliau* had been popular in France a century earlier, but Chaucer changed many of its features. Essentially *fabliau* was a versified short story designed to make you laugh, its subject matter often indecent, frequently about sexual or excretory functions! The debate has often centred around the position of the form in literary society, but it has been difficult to define precisely what was intended and who was the likely audience. *Fabliau* in France had largely died out by the time Chaucer was writing his versions in *The Canterbury Tales* (altogether seven of the stories fit the genre). Some have seen Chaucer's *fabliau* – which are coarse and realistic – as a bourgeois genre, contrasting with the refined and idealizing romance of courtly poetry. Others have staked a strong claim for Chaucer's *fabliau* being as courtly as the romance, recognizing what he added to the form by way of characterization, realism and description.

Focus on morality

Closely linked to the issues about the *fabliau* (which by its nature is 'indecent'), there has been a lot of discussion and consideration of morality and at the heart of any debate about morality is this question: is the tale simply a diverting romp (just a funny story) or does it contain serious moral messages? This discussion applies not just to *The Miller's Tale*, but also to the other *fabliaux* in *The Canterbury Tales*. One moral interpretation is that the tale has a framework of three basic temptations or sins, and that it stands as a paradigm (a kind of model) of punishments for these sins: lechery (Nicholas), avarice (John) and pride (Absolon).

Focus on the principles of life

In a sense this area of critical focus deals with *The Canterbury Tales* as a whole. Clearly the content and language of the Miller's story is very different to the Knight's and there is equally a variety amongst the other tales. A constant contrast with *The Knight's Tale* has regularly preoccupied critics, reminding us that there appear to be two different worlds that interested Chaucer early in the story-telling process. One was the idealized romantic and heroic setting portrayed by the Knight, a world full of true Christian virtues and conventional morality; the other the world of the Miller in a form of tale sometimes called 'festive comedy'. Inevitably critics have been interested in trying to find Chaucer's values in one or other of the contrasting interpretations of life. Bearing in mind the successful presentation of realism in this 'festive comedy' – how the everyday lives of ordinary people are presented, along with recognition of many of their basic desires and functions – the tale can be seen as a counterpoise to the lofty ideals of the Knight's values, summed up by one critic as 'the people's unofficial truth'. (A. David, *The Strumpet Muse: Art and Morals in Chaucer's Poetry*, Indiana University Press, 1976). This sees the tale as a bourgeois interpretation of life in which the common person is at the centre of events.

Examination of other principles: spiritual versus freedom of will

To extend this discussion a little further, it is worth recognizing that there is a tension in *The Miller's Tale* very similar to one of the overall debates about *The Canterbury Tales* as a whole. This has been expressed by critics as a ceaseless debate between the concept of destiny, or Providence, on the one hand and the pull of freedom of the will, or as one critic has put it: *persistent claims of natural appetite* in the *all-too real world* (P.G. Ruggiers, *The Art of The Canterbury Tales*, Madison, 1965). To return to a familiar theme, this tension can be seen in the context of the relationship with *The Knight's Tale*. It also figures prominently in the religious themes that are mocked in the tale. Although religion and morality are mocked in the parody of the flood, there is a tension throughout between extreme moral guidance (mainly in the dialogue between Nicholas and John) and the longings and fulfilment of natural sexual desire, which would conflict with the Christian messages.

The Canterbury Tales as a work is often considered in a similar way. Critics have commended Chaucer for his varied view of life. Throughout his tales he represents the natural instincts of fellow human beings just as strongly as he writes about spiritual concepts.

Examination of the burlesque of courtly idealism

It will come as no surprise to you to discover that critics have written a great deal about the courtly parody, and like all of these critical explorations, this is closely linked to the *fabliau* and the relationship with *The Knight's Tale*. Much of the ground has been covered in the Notes and Interpretations. Here are a few additional points: idealized love in a world where the standards of conduct are inappropriate; innuendoes and ironies connected with the use of music – remember that music would have been a fine accomplishment amongst courtly lovers – possibly contrasting the 'old song' of lust and cupidity with the 'new song' of grace; echoes in the language of popular poetry alongside biblical language from the *Song of Songs* (a series of poems that tell the story of two lovers: Solomon and a lady called the Shulamite woman; the book is almost entirely their own words, though just occasionally a few others add their own thoughts; it was written by Solomon and the events described took place around 965 BC, nearly 3,000 years ago).

Part of the study of burlesque (a satirical distortion) centres on the sexual undertones and connotations in the language and some critics have inevitably scrutinized this in detail. You would be advised to read the Notes to check on the double meanings and suggestiveness of some of the language, noting uses of the words *queynte*, *pryvetee*, *spille*, as well as the more explicit sexual language. Extending the point made above about the suggestions in the music, this has also been put forward as evidence of the bawdy burlesque: Nicholas's singing of *Angelus ad virginem* rather spicily foretells his own role in relation to Alison; and then there is the most celebrated religious musical moment in the poem, noticed by many critics as impeccably and explicitly timed to celebrate Nicholas's and Alison's love making:

> Ther was the revel and the melodye;
> And thus lith Alison and Nicholas,
> In bisynesse of myrthe and of solas,
> Til that the belle of laudes gan to rynge,
> And freres in the chauncel gonne synge. (544–548)

Who is the narrator?

Critics have had to ponder the no-man's land in terms of precisely who to ascribe the tale to. Bear in mind: the elaborate dialogue in *The Miller's Prologue*; Chaucer's own interventions; the views expressed at the beginning and end of the tale by the Reeve; the evident comparison with *The Knight's Tale*; the Miller's interruptions of his own tale; and *The Reeve's Prologue*, which generally accompanies *The Miller's Tale*.

Of course it is Chaucer himself who is at the centre of the whole work, ultimately as the author of all that is written or said. But Chaucer takes on two poses in *The Canterbury Tales*, one as the poet (where he stands back) and one as the pilgrim/poet, a role in which he speaks direct dialogue. His cleverness has commanded the attention of many critics. The tale itself is part of the game being played – the competition for the best story on the way to Canterbury and back to London – and there are important considerations about the structural arrangements. Critics have suggested that one reason why Chaucer 'gets away' with such a ribald tale is precisely because of the structure he imposes on the work as a whole, delegating the telling to the Miller, who he has already established as a scoundrel, linking him in a running squabble with the Reeve and contrasting his narrative and values with those belonging to the Knight. Chaucer himself can thus remain aloof from all the moral issues and any criticism of the bawdiness.

Essay Questions

Worked questions

The two questions below are followed by some ideas you might address in your response.

1   **Discuss the means by which humour is established in the tale. In your answer state whether the tale is simply humorous or whether it has a moral purpose.**

Here are some ideas you might explore in your response:

- The *Miller's Prologue* sets a tone of buffoonery through the descriptions of the Miller's behaviour before the tale itself starts.
- Bawdiness plays a major part in the proceedings. This happens early in the tale in the way that Nicholas woos Alison.
- Nicholas's elaborate hoax is farcical and needs exploring in detail. He maintains a total pretence through his play acting, which traps the hapless John.
- Absolon's foppish behaviour contributes to the mockery.
- The *fabliau* structure is both farcical and bawdy, and leads to the hilarious climax, which returns to John's expectation of the coming of a second flood.
- In spite of the humour there are themes of destiny and apparent justice and the characters are punished for their shortcomings. You would need to explore the significance of these themes and assess whether they are prominent enough to lend the tale a moral purpose.
- You may also wish to consider the dialogue between the Miller and the Reeve in *The Reeve's Prologue*. Does the irritation of the Reeve add to or detract from the humour?

2   **Choose any one of the four main characters. Consider in detail how the character is developed.**

Here are some ideas you might explore in your response:

- Explore how the pen portraits introduce the characters. Look in detail at how the attributes of the character are considered, for example how details of physical description and clothing are used.
- Discuss the styles of language used in the introductions or portraits.
- Consider the place of the character as a 'stock' character in the genre of *fabliau*.
- Conversely, make some judgements on the realistic elements within the characterization.
- What is the importance of characterization? Why is it essential that the character is presented in such detail?
- Explore ways in which the actions of the character link with and bear on his or her nature in the early parts of the tale.
- Assess the way that Chaucer deals with the destiny of the character. Is his or her fate justified?

Sample questions

The following questions are for you to try.

1 Explore the ways in which characters are mocked and made to look foolish.
2 Examine Chaucer's use of imagery in *The Miller's Tale*. You should write in detail about two or three selected passages in your answer.
3 From your understanding of the Miller in his prologue, does the tale appear to express his character? In what other ways are the themes and ideas of *The Miller's Prologue* developed in the tale?

4   In what ways is the characterization of Alison a parody of the courtly heroine?

5   Explore the techniques used by Chaucer to represent aspects of the real medieval world in the poem.

6   Discuss the extent to which each of the main characters receives their just deserts at the conclusion of the tale.

7   How important is the contrast between youth and age in the tale and how is it established by Chaucer?

8   Examine the importance of religion in the tale.

9   It is often noted that a strong feature of the style and structure of the tale is striking realism in an overall structure of fantasy. Discuss the effects of combining realism with fantasy.

10 Is Nicholas more a victim than a hero?

11 Examine in detail the theme of deception.

12 Consider the effectiveness and importance of the central incident in the tale (lines 311–548), which describes the cuckolding of John.

13 The style of the poem has been described as versatile. Comment on the range of styles used by Chaucer in *The Miller's Tale*.

14 In what ways does Chaucer interconnect the events and characters? To what extent do these connections contribute to the overall dramatic success of the tale?

15 Chaucer presents three very different male characters in *The Miller's Tale*. In what contrasting ways does he present masculinity?

16 Examine the role of the minor characters.

17 How far does its outrageous and bawdy language contribute to the success of *The Miller's Tale*?

18 How does Chaucer help to shape the reader's reaction to Absolon? Do you sympathize with him?

Chronology

1315–16	Great Famine
1321–2	Civil War in England
1327	Deposition and death of Edward II; accession of Edward III
1337	Start of the Hundred Years War
Early 1340s	Geoffrey Chaucer born, the son of John (a wine merchant) and Agnes – originally the family came from Ipswich
1346	Defeat of the French at Crècy
1348	Black Death
1350	Statute of Labourers' Act passed
1356–9	Chaucer becomes a page in the household of the Countess of Ulster
1359	Fought in the wars with France in the army of Prince Lionel
1360	Captured and ransomed
1360–6	Studied law and finance at the Inns of Court; 1361 second major occurrence of plague; 1362 *Piers Plowman* published
1366	Evidence of Chaucer travelling in Europe, possibly on a pilgrimage; married (Philippa); Chaucer's father died
1366–70	Chaucer travelled again in Europe, four times; destinations unknown but possibly including a journey to Italy; 1367 first record of Chaucer's membership of the royal household – a squire in the court
1368–72	*The Book of the Duchess* written in this period; before 1372 translated the *Roman de la Rose* (*The Romaunt of the Rose*)
1372–3	Chaucer on King's business in Italy

1374	Moved to Aldgate in London; appointed Customs Controller (to control taxes on wool, sheepskins, and leather)
1376–7	Further travelling in Flanders and France on King's secret business. In 1376 'Good Parliament' meets; death of Edward, the Black Prince. 1377 Death of Edward III; accession of Richard II
1378	Travelled again to Italy – renewed acquaintance with works of Italian writers
1378–80	*The House of Fame* written; 1379 Richard II introduces Poll Tax
1380–2	*The Parliament of Fowls* written; 1381 Peasants' Revolt
1380s	Chaucer moved to Kent (precise date unknown)
1382–6	*Troilus and Criseyde* and *The Legend of Good Women* written; 1385 gave up the post at Customs House; became Justice of the Peace
1386	Gave up house at Aldgate; election to Parliament
1387	Philippa presumed to have died
1388–92	The *General Prologue* and earlier *Canterbury Tales* written; 1389–91 appointed to be Clerk of the King's works. 1391–2 *A Treatise on the Astrolabe* written
1392–5	Most of *The Canterbury Tales* completed
1396–1400	Later *The Canterbury Tales* written; 1396 Anglo-French Treaty. 1397–9 Richard II's reign of 'tyranny'
1399	Chaucer returned to London, living in a house near the Lady Chapel of Westminster Abbey; deposition of Richard II; accession of Henry IV
1400	Chaucer died (date on tomb in Westminster Abbey given as 25 October)

Further Reading

Editions and commentaries

The following books have useful notes, especially those by Winny and Brewer:

L.D. Benson (ed.), *The Riverside Chaucer* (Oxford University Press, 1988).

Elisabeth Brewer, *The Miller's Tale* (Longman, 1982) York Notes.

T.W. Ross (ed.), '*The Miller's Tale*' (Norman, 1983), Volume II, part 3 of *A Variorum Edition of the Works of Geoffrey Chaucer*.

W.W. Skeat (ed.), *The Complete Works*, Volume V (Oxford University Press, 1900).

James Winny (ed.), *The Miller's Prologue and Tale* (Cambridge University Press, 1971).

Biography

D.R. Howard, *Chaucer, His Life, His Works, His World* (Dutton, New York, 1987).

G. Kane, *Chaucer* (Past Masters Series) (Oxford University Press, 1984).

D. Pearsall, *The Life of Geoffrey Chaucer* (Blackwell, 1992).

Criticism

J.A.W. Bennett, *Chaucer at Oxford and Cambridge* (Oxford University Press, 1974).

This article argues that *The Miller's Tale* is the source for the Flemish fabliau *Heile of Beersele* (see Appendix):

Frederick M. Biggs, 'The Miller's Tale and Heile van Beersele', *Review of English Studies*, 56 (2005), 497–523.

This book contains two essays on *The Canterbury Tales*; one by
Charles Muscatine, the other by Nevill Coghill:
D.S. Brewer (ed.), *Chaucer and Chaucerians* (Nelson, 1966).

This critical work prints and translates three analogues of *The
Miller's Tale*:
W.F. Bryan and G. Dempster (eds.), *Sources and Analogues of
    Chaucer's Canterbury Tales* (Chicago, 1941).

This chapter provides a guide to criticism of *The Miller's Tale*:
Helen Cooper, *The Canterbury Tales*, 2nd edition, *Oxford Guides
    to Chaucer* (Oxford University Press, 1996), pp. 92–107.

This book is still valuable on particular issues, though some of
its conclusions have been contested:
W.C. Curry, *Chaucer and the Medieval Sciences* (London, 1960).

This book, pp. 90–108, explains the place of *The Miller's Tale*
in *The Canterbury Tales*:
Alfred David, *The Strumpet Muse* (Indiana, 1976).

This essay discusses the Miller's parodies of medieval love
poetry:
E.T. Donaldson, 'The Miller's Tale' A3483–6, first published in
    A.S. Downer (ed.), *English Institute Essays* 1950 (Columbia,
    1951). It has been reprinted many times, notably in
    Donaldson's *Speaking of Chaucer* (Athlone, 1970).

This critical work brings Charles Muscatine's account of the
fabliau up to date:
J. Hines, *The Fabliau in English* (London, 1993).

This article relates elements of religious parody in the tale to its
recent political interpretations:
Andrew James Johnston, 'The Exegetics of Laughter: Religious
    Parody in Chaucer's *Miller's Tale*' in Manfred Pfister (ed.),
    A History of English Laughter (Rodopi, 2002).

This book discusses the action of the first five *Canterbury Tales*
in the light of contemporary visual materials:
V.A. Kolve, *Chaucer and the Imagery of Narrative* (London, 1984).

This article investigates bodies, gender stereotypes and fourteenth-century fashions in clothing in the tale:
Linda Lomperis, 'Bodies that Matter in the Court of Late Medieval England and in Chaucer's *Miller's Tale*', *Romantic Review*, 86 (1995), 243–64.

This is still the best book on Chaucer and contains an interesting discussion of *fabliau* (pp. 58–71). You will also find a very influential chapter on the style of *The Miller's Tale* (pp. 223–30):
Charles Muscatine, *Chaucer and the French Tradition* (California, 1957).

This book provides a Marxist reading of *The Miller's Tale*:
Lee Patterson, *Chaucer and the Subject of History* (Routledge, 1991).

This book, pp. 166–83, provides an excellent critical account of the issues in the tale:
D. Pearsall, *The Canterbury Tales* (Unwin, 1985).

This article analyses the significance of references to the Mystery Plays in *The Miller's Tale*:
Sandra Pierson Prior, 'Parodying Typology and the Mystery Plays in *The Miller's Tale*', *Journal of Medieval and Renaissance Studies* 16 (1986), 57–73.

This chapter provides a guide to criticism of *The Miller's Tale*:
Thomas W. Ross, 'Survey of Criticism' in *The Miller's Tale*, (University of Oklahoma Press, 1983) Volume II, part 3 of *A Variorum Edition of the Works of Geoffrey Chaucer*.

This book contains a helpful essay on *fabliau* tales – 'The Fabliaux' by D.S. Brewer:
Beryl Rowland (ed.), *Companion to Chaucer Studies* (Oxford University Press, 1968).

This book provides a feminist critique of male fantasies concerning Alison's sexuality:
Elaine Tuttle Hansen, *Chaucer and the Fictions of Gender* (University of California Press, 1992).

This page gives access to a range of excellent teaching and scholarly materials on Chaucer:
www.courses.fas.edu/~chaucer/index.htm

This page of the Luminarium website gives access to critical essays on *The Miller's Tale*:
www.luminarium.org/medlit/miller.htm

Language

D. Burnley, *A Guide to Chaucer's Language* (Methuen, 1983).
N. Davis (ed.), *A Chaucer Glossary* (Oxford University Press, 1968).

A Note on Chaucer's English

Chaucer's English has so many similarities with Modern English that it is unnecessary to learn extensive tables of grammar. With a little practice, and using the glosses provided, it should not be too difficult to read the text. Nevertheless, it would be foolish to pretend that there are no differences. The remarks which follow offer some information, hints and principles to assist students who are reading Chaucer's writings for the first time, and to illustrate some of the differences (and some of the similarities) between Middle and Modern English. More comprehensive and systematic treatments of this topic are available in *The Riverside Chaucer* and in D. Burnley, *A Guide to Chaucer's Language*.

1 Inflections

These are changes or additions to words, usually endings, which provide information about number (whether a verb or a noun is singular or plural), tense or gender.

a) Verbs

In the **present** tense most verbs add –e in the first person singular (e.g. *I ryde*), –est in the second person singular (e.g. *thou sayest*), –eth in the third person singular (*she sayeth*) and –en in the plural. This can be summarized as follows:

	Middle English	Modern English
Singular	1 I telle 2 Thou tellest 3 He/She/It telleth	I tell You tell He/She/It tells
Plural	1 We tellen 2 Ye tellen 3 They tellen	We tell You tell They tell

As you can see, Middle English retains more inflections than Modern English, but the system is simple enough. Old English, the phase of the language between around 449 AD, when the Angles first came to Britain, and about 1100, had many more inflections.

In describing the **past** tense it is necessary to begin by making a distinction, which still applies in Modern English, between strong and weak verbs. **Strong verbs** form their past tense by changing their stem (e.g. I sing, I sang; you drink, you drank; he fights, he fought; we throw, we threw), while **weak verbs** add to the stem (I want, I wanted; you laugh, you laughed; he dives, he dived).

In the past tense in Middle English, strong verbs change their stems (e.g. *sing* becomes *sang* or *song*) and add –e in the second person singular (e.g. *thou songe*) and –en in the plural (e.g. *they songen*). Weak verbs add –de or –te (e.g. *fele* becomes *felte*, *here* becomes *herde*) with –st in the second person singular (e.g. *thou herdest*) and –n in the plural (e.g. *they felten*). The tables below and on the next page compare the past tense in Middle and Modern English for strong and weak verbs.

Strong verbs		
	Middle English Present stem: 'sing'	**Modern English**
Singular	1 I sange (or soonge) 2 Thou songe 3 He/She/It sange	I sang (or sung) You sang He/She/It sang
Plural	1 We songen 2 Ye songen 3 They songen	We sang You sang They sang

Weak verbs		
	Middle English Present stem: 'here'	**Modern English**
Singular	1 I herde 2 Thou herdest 3 He/She/It herde	I heard You heard He/She/It heard
Plural	1 We herden 2 Ye herden 3 They herden	We heard You heard They heard

The past tense can also be formed using the auxiliary verb Gan plus the past participle (e.g. *gan... dresse* (line 360): went, *gan wype* (line 622): wiped). Gan sometimes means 'began' in phrases involving the preposition 'to' (e.g. *gan to rynge* (line 547): began to ring) but even in some of these cases past tense is required (e.g. *gan to stele* (line 678): stole, went). Some verbs add initial y to make their past participle (e.g. *ytoold* (line 1): told, *ydight* (line 97): adorned).

b) Nouns and adjectives

Nouns mostly add –s or –es for plural (e.g. *songes* [line 223]) and possessive (e.g. *wrightes* [line 35]), but notice *carpenteris* [line 235], *carpenteres* [line 248]. There are no apostrophes in Middle English! (But modern editors sometimes add one to indicate that a letter has been elided, e.g. M'*athynketh* (line 62). Some nouns add -en for plural (e.g. *eyen* [line 209]). Although (unlike modern French or German) nouns do not take grammatical gender in Middle English, some nouns add –e for feminine (e.g. *tappestere* barmaid [line 228]). Some adjectives add –e in the plural. Some adjectives are converted to adverbs by the addition of –e (e.g. *faire* [line 181]: graciously).

c) Personal pronouns

The forms of the personal pronouns are somewhat different from those used in Modern English and are worth recording in full:

		Subject	Object	Possessive
Singular	1	I, ich	me	myn, my
	2	Thou, thow	thee	thyn, thy
	3 masculine	He	hym, him	his
	3 feminine	She	her	hir, hire
	3 neuter	It, hit	it, hit	his
Plural	1	We	us	owre, our, owres
	2	Ye	you, yow	your, youres
	3	They	hem	hire, here

Remember that the distinction between *thou* and *you* in Middle English often involves politeness and social relationship as well as number. This is similar to modern French or German. Thus *thou* forms are used with friends, family and social inferiors, *you* forms with strangers or superiors. There are occasions when changes between the forms seem to indicate a change in the speaker's attitude to the person addressed (as in Absolon's speeches at the window (lines 590–681, 684–97)), but in other places it is hard to detect any significance in the change (e.g. lines 176–79).

2 Relative pronouns

The main **relative pronouns** found are *that* and *which*. In translating *that* it is often wise to try out a range of Modern English equivalents, such as *who, whom, which*. The prefix *ther-* in such words as *therto* and *therwith* often refers back to the subject matter of the previous phrase. *Therto* may be translated as 'in addition to all that' or 'in order to achieve that'.

3 Impersonal construction

With certain verbs the **impersonal construction** is quite common (e.g. *hym leste* [line 313]: it pleased him, *Me reweth* [line 354]): it saddens me, *M'athynketh* [line 62]: it seems to me, *nedeth nat enquere* [line 58]: there is no need to ask).

4 Reflexive pronouns

Many verbs can be used with a **reflexive pronoun**, a pronoun which refers back to the subject (as in modern French or German) and which may, depending on the verb employed, be translated or understood as part of the verb (e.g. *dressed hym* [line 250]: placed himself, *shapen hym* [line 295]: devise, *blessen hym* [line 340]: cross himself).

5 Extra negatives

In Middle English extra **negatives** often make the negative stronger, whereas in Modern English double negatives cancel each other out. *Ther nys no man* (line 145) would now be 'there is no man', *I nam no labbe* (line 401) 'I am no tell-tale'. Lines 309–10 present a more complicated case.

> For, for no cry hir mayde koude hym calle,
> He nolde answere for thyng that myghte falle.

This means 'in spite of any cry her maid could make to him, he would not answer, whatever happened.'

6 Contraction

Sometimes negatives and pronouns merge with their associated verbs (e.g. *noot* [= *ne woot*] [line 556]: did not know, *knowestow* [line 48]: do you know, *artow* [line 49]: are you).

7 Word order

Middle English **word order** is often freer than Modern English, and in particular there is more inversion of subject and verb (e.g.

Crul was his heer (line 206) or subject and object (e.g. *A brooch she baar* [line 157]). In analysing difficult sentences you should first locate the verb, then its subject, then the object or complement. (Roughly, a verb which involves activity takes an object – she hit the ball, he gave her the book – while a verb which describes a state of affairs takes a complement – it was yellow, you look better.) Then you should put these elements together. It should then be easier to see how the various qualifiers fit in.

In the sentence beginning at line 433, the main verbs are 'be' and 'hadde had'. By putting them together with their subjects and complements we reach 'he had rather that she had had a ship'. Then we can find places for the qualifiers: 'I dare well say that at that time *he would rather* than all his black male sheep *that she had had a ship* for herself alone.'

Chaucer sometimes adds to his sentences in ways that you might be criticized for. For example the second sentence of the tale keeps elaborating on Nicholas's skill at astrology and the kinds of questions people might ask him, until the poet gives up on the sentence: 'With him was living a poor scholar, who had studied arts but preferred to concentrate on astrology, and knew some of the propositions such as how to determine by looking at the stars, if men should ask him, whether it would rain or be dry at a certain time, or if they asked him what should happen in some other matter; I cannot recount all possible cases.' Any modern English teacher would make three or four sentences out of this, but perhaps Chaucer achieves an effect by allowing the sentence to meander on.

Extra qualifications can make short sentences harder to unravel. In the sentence beginning at line 642, the main idea (in lines 643–4) is fairly easy to grasp: 'I would rather than all this town that I should be avenged for this insult.' But the addition of another expression complicates the idea: 'May I give my soul to Satan if I would not rather than all this town be avenged for this insult.'

8 Connection of clauses

Middle English often does not indicate **connection of clauses** as clearly as Modern English. In seeking to understand or in translating you may need to provide connecting words (as I did in the discussion of the second sentence of the tale above). On occasion you may have to provide verbs which have been omitted (particularly the verb 'to be', e.g. *Hir filet brood of silk* [line 135]: Her broad headband was made of silk, or verbs of motion) or regularize number or tense (in some Middle English sentences a subject can shift from singular to plural or a verb from present to past).

Chaucer can mix the past tense with the historic present (sometimes in telling a story we use the present tense, even though we and our audience know that the events occurred in the past) but a Modern English writer would have to maintain consistency at least within the sentence and usually within the paragraph as well. Chaucer's usage here (and with the implied words and the lack of connectives) may well be closer to spoken English than modern formal writing could be.

9 Change of meaning

Although most of the words which Chaucer uses are still current (often with different spellings) in Modern English, some of them have changed their meaning. (All the words in the first sentence of *The Miller's Prologue* exist in Modern English, but the modern meanings of *namely, route* [=rout] and *gentil* [=gentle] would be inappropriate here.) So it is a good idea to check the Notes or the Glossary even for words which look familiar. If you are interested in investigating the ways in which words change their meanings over time you can look at the quotations provided in large historical dictionaries, such as the *Oxford English Dictionary* or the *Shorter Oxford Dictionary* or in R.W. Burchfield, *The English Language* (Oxford, 1985), pp. 113–23, or G. Hughes, *Words in Time: A Social History of*

English Vocabulary (Blackwell). Some more examples from *The Miller's Tale* are shown in the following table.

Middle English word	(line number)	Meaning	Equivalent modern word
barge	(442)	ship, sea-going vessel	barge
cast	(497)	trick	cast
celle	(714)	floor	cell
chambre	(95)	bedroom	chamber
cheere	(510)	expression	cheer
child	(217)	young man, lad	child
chippes	(640)	woodchips	chips
clerk	(91)	student, learned man	clerk
conseil	(395, 422)	secret, advice	counsel
daungerous	(230)	fastidious	dangerous
deffie	(650)	denounce	defy
drenchen	(509)	drown	drench
estaat	(121)	position in society, status	estate, state
filet	(135)	headband	fillet
fyndyng	(112)	provision, gifts	findings
gentil	(63)	noble, highborn, virtuous	gentle

A Note on Pronunciation

The Miller's Tale, like other poems, benefits from being read aloud. Even if you read it aloud in a Modern English pronunciation you will get more from it, but Middle English was pronounced differently (the sounds of a language change over time at least as much as the vocabulary or the constructions) and it helps to make some attempt at a Middle English accent. The best way to learn this is to imitate one of the recordings (the tapes issued by Pavilion and Argo are especially recommended for this purpose). A few principles are given below; more can be found in *The Riverside Chaucer*.

1   In most cases you should pronounce all consonants (for example you should sound the 'k' in knight and the 'l' in half). But in words of French origin initial 'h' (as in *hostelrye* (line 95) for example) should not be sounded, nor should 'g' in the combination 'gn'. The combination 'gh' (as in *droghte* [line 88]) is best sounded 'ch' as in Scottish 'loch'.

2   In most cases all vowels are sounded, though a final 'e' may be silent because of elision with a vowel following (e.g. do not sound the second 'e' in *seyde it* [line 3]) or because of the stress pattern of the line (e.g. I would sound the final 'e' in *quite* [line 11], but leave it silent in *Millere* [line 12]).

3   Two points of spelling affect pronunciation. When 'y' appears as a vowel you should sound it as 'i' (see table on page 182). Sometimes a 'u' sound before 'n' or 'm' was written 'o' (because 'u' and 'n' looked very similar in the handwriting of the time). This means that *song* and *yong* should be pronounced 'sung' and 'yung'. This also applies in *comen* and *sonne* (as in their Modern English equivalents 'come' and 'son').

4 You will not go too far wrong with combinations of vowels, such as *ai*, *eu* and *oy* if you sound them as in Modern English. There are significant exceptions (for example *mous* (line 238) and *hous* (line 248) and many words of similar ending should be pronounced with an *oo* sound) but it is not possible to establish reliable rules purely on the basis of the spelling.

5 The principal vowel sounds differ somewhat from Modern English. They are set out in the table below (adapted from Norman Davis's table in *The Riverside Chaucer*). The table distinguishes long and short versions of each vowel. This distinction still applies in Modern English (consider the 'a' sounds in hat and father) but unfortunately it is often only possible to decide whether a particular vowel is long or short by knowing about the derivation of the word. Do not despair. Even a rough approximation will help you. Only experts in medieval languages have reliable Middle English accents, and even they cannot be sure that Chaucer would have approved them.

Vowel	Middle English example (line numbers given in brackets)	Modern equivalent sound
Long 'a'	cas (163), stable (464)	'a' in father
Short 'a'	sat (13), nat (24)	'a' in hat
Long 'e'	he (3), been (46)	'a' in fate
Open 'e'	heeth (154), teche (491)	'e' in there
Short 'e'	gent (126), wende (585)	'e' in set
Unstressed 'e'	nones (18), sonne (314)	'a' in about, 'e' in forgotten
Long 'i'	I (6), tyme (111)	'i' in machine
Short 'i'	hym (82), aright (7)	'i' in sit
Long 'o'	no (15), moot (6)	'o' in note
Open 'o'	hooly (400), goon (445)	'oa' in broad
Short 'o'	som (344), solas (92)	'o' in hot
Long 'u'	doute (453), mous (238)	'oo' in boot
Short 'u'	But (29), ful (46)	'u' in put

Glossary

This glossary is not absolutely comprehensive. It does not record all inflected forms (see A Note on Chaucer's English, pp. 173–5) nor all variant spellings. If you do not find a word here, try sounding it out, or try minor modifications of spelling (such as 'i' for 'y', 'a' for 'o', 'ea' for 'ee', and vice versa). Generally the main meaning in this text comes first, while more specialized meanings are given line references. Proper names which are explained in the Notes do not appear in the glossary. In compiling this glossary I have relied on L.D. Benson (ed.), *The Riverside Chaucer* and on N. Davis (ed.), *A Chaucer Glossary*, which offer fuller explanations than I can here. I have also consulted the *Oxford English Dictionary* and *The Middle English Dictionary*.

aboute   around
abyd   wait
abyde   defer to (line 15)
accorded   agreed
acordaunt   in harmony with
acquitance   release of property
adrad   afraid
affeccioun   love, emotion
after   according to (line 112), about (line 554)
agast   afraid
agayn   again, towards, back
al   all, entirely
Almageste   astronomy textbook (see Notes p. 53, line 100)
also   as
amydde   in the middle of
amys   wrongly
anon   at once
a-nyghtes   at night
apart   apart, on their own
ape   fool
apeyren   injure

aright   well
arraieth   dresses
array   condition, preparation
art   the arts course (see Notes p. 51, line 83), astronomy (line 101)
art   are
artow   are you
aslake   slacken, diminish, go down
astrelabie   astrolabe
astrologye   astrology (see Notes p. 51, line 84)
astromye   astronomy
aswowne   in a faint, unconscious
athynketh   it displeases
atones   at once
atwo   in two, apart
atwynne   apart
augrym   stones, counting stones
availleth   benefits, profits
avalen   take off

avyseth consider
awook awoke
axed asked
ay always
ayens against, compared with

bad advised, commanded, told
balkes beams
barge boat, ship
barmclooth apron
barred striped
benedicitee bless
bent curved, arched
berne barn
bet better
biddeth prays, requests
bifalle happen
bifel happened
bifoore in front
biforn before
bigonne began
bigyle deceive
bileve creed
biseche ask
biset employ, bestow, place
bisynesse occupation, activity
bitake commend
blake black
blisful delightful
bokeler small shield
boldely confidently,
    immediately (line 325)
boos boss
bord board, stay
bord plank
bour bedroom
bragot bragget (an alcoholic
    drink made by fermenting ale
    and honey)
brawn muscle

brest breast, chest
brewhous pub
brocage use of an agent
brokkynge warbling, trilling
brood wide
brosten broken
broyden embroidered
bryd bird
bukke buck, male deer
but if unless

caped stared
capying staring
care trouble
carl rogue
cas event, occurrence, situation,
    chance
cast trick
casten leap, fling
Catoun *Cato* (elementary
    reader)
celle floor
certes certainly
certeyn certain, some, exact, a
    particular
cetewale setwall, zedoary (a
    spice resembling ginger)
ceynt belt
chambre bedroom
chartre charter, legal document
chauncel chancel
chaunteth sings
cheere expression, appearance
cherl churl, rascal
chese choose
child lad
chippes woodchips
chymenee fireplace, hearth
clappe chatter
cleped called

clerk   student, learned man (see Notes p. 52, line 91, p. 63, line 204)

clippe   cut

cloisterer   monk

clom   quiet, silent

clomben   climbed

cokewold   cuckold, betrayed husband

col-black   black, coalblack

cole   coal

coler   collar

comandement   command, disposal

compaignye   company, companions

conclusiouns   propositions

conseil   secret, advice (line 422)

cop   top

corde   rope

cors   body, corpse

corven   cut out

couched   placed

cride   shouted

crouche   make the sign of the cross

crul   curly

curteisie   courtesy

dame   mother

daun   master

debaat   quarrel, argument

dede   dead

deede   action

deel   part

deere   precious

deerelyng   darling

deerne   secret

defame   defame, spoil someone's reputation

deffie   denounce

demen   judge, decide, believe, think

depe   deeply

devel   devil

devocioun   devotion, prayer

deye   die

disporte   enjoy

doke   duck

doute   doubt, fear

drawen   to impress on (line 4)

drenche   drown

dresse   prepare, put on clothes, direct attention to (line 360)

dressed   placed (line 250)

dreynt   drowned, submerged

droghte   drought, dry weather

dronke   drunk, drunken

dronken   being drunk

drough   drew

drow   drew

echon   each one, all

eek   also, moreover (line 448)

eft   again

eftsoones   immediately, another time

eir   air

elde   old age

elles, ellis   else, otherwise

elves   evil spirits

enquere   ask, investigate

entente   intention, purpose

er   before

ernest   serious, seriousness

ers   arse

erys   ears

esily   easily, gently

espye   see, notice

estaat   position in society, status

evere ever, always
everichon everyone, all of them
everideel every part, all of it
eyle ail, be wrong with

fair beautiful
faire beautifully, neatly (line 102), properly (line 460)
faldyng coarse woollen cloth
falsen falsify
fantasye imagination, desire, delusion
faste rapidly, vigorously, hard, securely (line 391)
fecche fetch
felaweshipe companions
fer far
ferde fared, acted, did
ferre farther
fetisly handsomely, elegantly
fey faith, honour
fil happened, began
filet headband
fle fly
foo foe, enemy
foond found, tried
for because of (line 12), in spite of, out of respect for (line 60)
forbere restrain
forlore utterly lost, damned
foyson plenty
freres friars
froteth rubs, chafes
ful very
fyndyng provision, gifts

gabbe talk excessively
game play, joke
gan was

gan to began to
gauren stare
gay elegant, delightful, bright, fine
gaylard lively
gent delicate
gentil noble, fine
gentillesse noble behaviour (see Notes p. 47, line 63)
gentils those of noble birth
gesse imagine, suppose
gestes lodgers
giterne gittern, stringed instrument (see Notes p. 64, line 225)
gleede embers
gnof churl, lout
goliardeys buffoon, joker
gon go, prosper (line 6)
goore fold, flounce
goost spirit, soul
gooth goes
grace mercy, forgiveness
gracious pleasing, attractive
grange granary, farm building
greet, grete great, large, long
greyn cardamom seed
gyternynge gittern-playing

haaf heaved
haliday holy day
halves sides
harlotrye crude stories, ribald talk
harm injury, wrong
harre hinges
harwed harrowed, plundered
haspe fastenings, hinges
hastif urgent
haunchebones thighs

heed head, mind, thoughts (line 420)
heeld kept
heeled healed
heeng hung
heer hair
heeste command
heeth heather
hem them
hende courteous, handy (see Notes p. 52, line 91)
hente seize, pounce
herestow do you hear?
herkneth listen
herneys equipment, clothing
herte heart
herys hairs
heve raise, lift
hewe colouring, complexion
hidous dreadful
hir, hire their
hir, hire her
hoolynesse holiness
hoor grey-haired
hoord store
hooste host
hoot hot
hopen dance
hors horse
hoses stockings
hostelrye lodging-house, large house, inn
hust hush, be quiet
hye high

icched itched
ich I
ilke same
impressioun impression (see Notes p. 84, lines 503–05)

in house (especially lodging-house)
inquisityf inquisitive, curious
interrogaciouns questions

jalous jealous
janglere chatterer, teller of tales
jape joke
jolif, joly pretty, high-spirited, frisky, lively, full of desire (line 247)
jubbe jug

kan know
kembeth combs
kers cress
kiked stared
kirtel tunic
knarre rugged man
knave servant
knedyng kneading
knowestow you know
konne know how to
koude understood
kymelyn kimlin, trough (see Notes p. 79, line 440)

labbe tell-tale, chatterbox
lat let
lat be stop, give up
latoun latten, brass
laudes lauds
leef page
leeste least
leet left, stopped
leeve, leve dear, beloved (line 285)
legende story, biography
leggen lay
lemman love, darling
lendes loins

lene lend
lese lose
leste pleased
levere rather, dearer
lewed ignorant, lascivious
leyser opportunity
lief dear
light cheerful, glad
lightnesse agility
lik like
likerous lustful, delightful, attractive
list wish
lith lie
litherly badly
longynge belonging (line 101)
loore learning
lorn lost, destroyed
loth disliked
lough laughed
love-longynge passionate desire
lovely loving
lycorys liquorice
lyf life, biography, life story of a saint (line 33)

madde go mad (lines 48, 451)
maistrye skill
maladye sickness
male bag
manere manner(s), way, kind of (line 573)
marle-pit clay pit
mateere subject-matter
mayden virgin (of either sex)
meede reward, money
meenes middlemen
meeth mead
meke gentle, submissive
merveyle wonder

mete food
mette dreamed
mislay lay wrongly
mo more
mooder mother
moorne mourn
moot might, may, must
moralitee moral teaching
morne morning
mowe may
mowled gone mouldy
mullok rubbish
myrie tuneful, happy
mysspeke say anything wrong

nam am not
namely especially
narwe closely (line 116)
nas was not
nat not
ne not, nor
nede need, necessity
nedeth it is necessary
newe new, recently (line 113)
noble coin (worth one third of a pound sterling) (line 148)
noght not, nothing
nolde would not, do not want
nones occasion
noon none, not one
noot do not know
nosethirles nostrils
nye near-by
nyght-spel night charm (see Notes p. 74, line 372)
nys is not
nyste did not know

o one
offrynge offering

oon one
ooth oath
ordinance command

paas pace
paramours love, lovemaking, lovers
pardee by God, certainly
parfay by my faith
passeth continues
passioun suffering (especially the suffering of Christ on the cross)
Pater-noster (Latin) 'Our Father', The Lord's Prayer
pere-jonette early ripening pear
perled decorated with beads
pich pitch
piggesnye pig's eye (a flower)
pipyng whistling
pleye frolic, amuse oneself, joke (see Notes p. 88, line 578)
plogh plough, ploughteam (line 51)
poke bag
popelote pet, little doll
poure poor
poynt-devys carefully, to the last detail
poyntes laces
preche preach
presse cupboard
preye beg, ask
privee discreet, secretive
prively secretly
profred offered
propre beautiful
proprely neatly
protestacioun solemn declaration
prye observe

pryme about nine a.m.
prymerole primrose
pryvetee secrets, private parts (see Notes p. 46, line 56)
purveiance preparations, foresight
pyment spiced wine

quake tremble
queynte sly (line 167), elegant, pleasing thing (see Notes p. 60, line 168), elaborate (line 497)
quite, quyte reply to, repay, rival
quod said
quynyble high treble

rage sport (with a sexual sense)
rated scolded
rathe early
raughte reached
reed red
reed advice (line 419)
reherce relate, repeat
rekene count
remenant rest
rente income
reve reeve, estate-manager
revel merriment
rewe take pity
rist rose
roghte care
rometh roams, makes his way
ronges rungs
route, rowte company
routeth snores
rubible rebec, a small two-stringed fiddle
rude uneducated, ignorant
rys bough

saugh saw
sautrie psaltery (a stringed instrument)
scaffold platform
scape escape
scole school, style
scoler scholar
se see
seken seek
sely simple, unfortunate, foolish
sencer censer (vessel containing incense)
sensynge spreading incense
sermonyng preaching
sette sit, place
seyde said
seye say, mean (line 497)
seyl sail
seyn say
seystow do you say
shapen devise, form
shette shut, locked
shilde forbid
shode parting (of hair)
shoon shone
shot-wyndowe hinged window (see Notes p. 66, line 250)
shour shower, rain
sik sigh
sikerly, sikirly certainly, indeed
simylitude likeness
sith since
sleigh sly, cunning
sloo sloe-berry
slye crafty
smal small, short, slender (line 126), delicately (line 212), high-pitched (line 252)
smale finely
smert pain

smok shift, slip
smoot struck
smyth blacksmith
smythed made, repaired
so as long as, provided that
softe discreetly, quietly
solas pleasure, delight, entertainment
somdeel somewhat
somwhat something
sond sand
song sung
soore bitterly, sorely
sooth truth
soothly truly
sorwe sorrow, trouble
soster sister
soun sound
Southwerk Southwark
sowne play, sound
spak spoke
spak agayn replied
speed hurry, succeed
spille die
spitously loudly, vehemently
sproong leaped, sprang
sprynge break (line 566)
squaymous squeamish
stalkes uprights
stalketh creeps
stant stands
stele handle (line 677)
stele creep (line 678)
sterte awoke, leaped
stille quietly, silent
stirynge moving
stondeth stands
stoon stone
storial historical
stree straw

stroke, strook blow
strouted spread out
sturdily resolutely, boldly
stynt stop
suffisant enough
suffiseth be satisfied
surplys robe
suyte pattern
swalwe swallow
swelte melt
swete sweat (line 594)
swich such
swogh groan
swoote sweet
swymme float
swynke labour, toil
syn since

tale story, words, talk
tapes ribbons
tappestere barmaid
tarie remain, delay
tariying delay
tasseled adorned with tassels
teche teach
tete teat
thakked patted
thenche think, imagine
ther there, where
therto in addition, for that purpose
therupon on top of it
therwithal besides, also, at that (line 260)
thikke thickly, sturdy
thilke that same
tho at that time, then
tho those
thonder-dent thunderclap
thresshfold threshold

thriftily properly, fittingly
throte throat
thy your
tikel unstable
til to
toucheth concerns, treats
tour tower
toute, towte buttocks
tow flax
travaille suffering
trave frame for horses
trewe true, wise (line 421), faithful (line 501)
trewe-love herb paris (line 584)
trewely truly
trippe dance
trogh trough
trouthe troth, pledged word
trowe think, believe
turned directed
turtel turtle-dove
tweye two

unbokeled unbuckled, opened
underspore lever (from below)
undertake promise
unnethe hardly
until to (line 653)
untold uncounted

vengeaunce punishment, revenge
verraily truly
verray true
viritoot (see Notes p. 93, line 662)
vitaille victuals, food and drink
voluper cap

wafres cakes
waget sky-blue

wake stay up, remain awake
walwynge rolling, surging
war aware
warante swear, wager
wayte watch, watch for, await
weel well
wel well, much
wenche lower-class woman,
    woman of loose morals,
    womanservant (line 523)
wende thought
wentestow did you go?
werede wore
werken act
werkes works, deeds
werte wart
wether male sheep
wey way
wey name (line 26)
weylawey alas
wezele weasel
whan when
whilom once
whit white
whoso whoever
wight creature, person
wille will, desires
wirche perform, do, work
wiste knew
wit reason, mind
wite know
withinne inside
withoute outside
wo sorrow, sadness, pain
wol will
wolle wool
wont accustomed
wood mad
woodnesse madness
woot know

woweth woos
wreye betray
wright carpenter
wrooth angry
wryed twisted
wyf woman, wife
wyle trick, stratagem
wynsynge skittish, lively
wyte blame

yaf gave
ybete beaten
yblent blinded
yborn carried
yclad dressed
ycleped called
ycrowe crowed
ydight decorated, arranged
ye eye (line 136)
ye you
yeman yeoman, free-born man
yerne lively
yeve give
yforged made, minted
ygeten got, obtained
ygrave engraved
yheere hear, heard
yleyd stowed away
ymaginacioun imagination
ynogh, ynowe enough
yong young
yoore formerly, long ago
yow you
ypulled plucked
yqueynt quenched
ysworn sworn
ytoold told
yvel evil, badly
ywis indeed

Appendix

The description of the Clerk

Compare this description from the *General Prologue* with the Miller's description of Nicholas (lines 91–112). How are the two descriptions organized? What are the differences between the two students? The comparison can reflect both the literary traditions of describing students (explored by Jill Mann in her *Chaucer and Medieval Estates Satire*, Cambridge, 1973), and the links between the pilgrim audience and the stories they hear.

285 A CLERK ther was of Oxenford also,
    That unto logyk hadde longe ygo.
    As leene was his hors as is a rake,
    And he nas nat right fat, I undertake,
    But looked holwe, and therto sobrely.
290 Ful thredbare was his overeste courtepy,
    For he hadde geten hym yet no benefice,
    Ne was so worldly for to have office.
    For hym was levere have at his beddes heed
    Twenty bookes, clad in blak or reed,
295 Of Aristotle and his philosophie
    Than robes riche, or fithele, or gay sautrie.
    But al be that he was a philosophre,
    Yet hadde he but litel gold in cofre;
    But al that he myghte of his freendes hente,
300 On bookes and on lernynge he it spente,
    And bisily gan for the soules preye
    Of hem that yaf hym wherwith to scoleye.
    Of studie took he moost cure and moost heede.
    Noght o word spak he moore than was neede,
305 And that was seyd in forme and reverence,
    And short and quyk and ful of hy sentence;
    Sownynge in moral vertu was his speche,
    And gladly wolde he lerne and gladly teche.

General Prologue 285–308

290 **overeste courtepy** short overcoat 291 **benefice** job in the
church 296 **fithele** a fiddle 297–8 The joke depends on the fact
that 'philosopher' could mean 'alchemist, one who devotes himself
to making gold'. 299 **hente** receive 302 **scoleye** attend
university 303 **cure** care 307 **Sownynge** in accord with

The description of the courtly lady

This is an example of the detailed description of a courtly lady,
parodied by Chaucer in his description of Alison (lines 125–62).
Notice the detailed part-by-part description and the comparison
with valuable or courtly objects. This example is the description of
Idleness from Chaucer's translation of the *Roman de la Rose* (lines
539–61), a thirteenth-century French poem describing the whole
art of love, written by Guillaume de Lorris and Jean de Meun. The
medieval manuals of poetry provided instructions for producing
this type of description (for example, Geoffrey de Vinsauf, *Poetria
nova*, lines 562–99) and Chaucer provides another fine example in
his youthful work *The Book of the Duchess*, lines 817–1041.

> Hir heer was as yelowe of hewe
540 As ony basyn scoured newe,
> Hir flesh tendre as is a chike,
> With bente browis smothe and slyke.
> And by mesure large were
> The openyng of hir yen clere,
545 Hir nose of good proporcioun,
> Hir yen grey as is a faucoun,
> With swete breth and wel savoured,
> Hir face whit and wel coloured,
> With litel mouth and round to see.
550 A clove chynne eke hadde she.
> Hir nekke was of good fasoun
> In lengthe and gretnesse, by resoun,
> Withoute bleyne, scabbe, or royne;
> Fro Jerusalem unto Burgoyne

555   Ther nys a fairer nekke, iwys,
       To fele how smothe and softe it is;
       Hir throte, also whit of hewe
       As snowe on braunche snowed newe.
       Of body ful wel wrought was she;
560   Men neded not in no cuntre
       A fairer body for to seke.

542   **slyke** sleek   551 **fasoun** fashion, shape
553   **bleyne** blemish; **royne** roughness
554   **Burgoyne** Burgundy

The behaviour of the courtly lover

This extract from *The Franklin's Tale* (lines 729–43) describes the wooing of the ideal courtly lover. This is parodied in different ways in *The Miller's Tale* in the behaviour of Nicholas and Absolon (lines 163–84, 231–88). Notice the emphasis on the suffering of the lover, on the great enterprises he undertakes in order to win his love, the lady's recognition of his worthiness and her pity for his suffering. There is another admirable description of the behaviour of the lover in *The Book of the Duchess* (lines 1088–297).

       In Armorik, that called is Britayne,
730   Ther was a knyght that loved and dide his payne
       To serve a lady in his beste wise;
       And many a labour, many a greet emprise,
       He for his lady wroghte er she were wonne.
       For she was oon the faireste under sonne,
735   And eek therto comen of so heigh kynrede
       That wel unnethes dorste this knyght, for drede,
       Telle hire his wo, his peyne, and his distresse.
       But atte laste she, for his worthynesse,
       And namely for his meke obeysaunce,
740   Hath swich a pitee caught of his penaunce

That pryvely she fil of his accord
To take hym for hir housbonde and hir lord,
Of swich lordshipe as men han over hir wyves.

734 **oon the faireste** the fairest   735 **kynrede** family
740 **penaunce** distress, suffering

Two examples of the *fabliau*

The Miller's Tale belongs to the medieval genre of the *fabliau* (described in the Notes on pp. 49–50). The two plot summaries which follow are intended to give a flavour of this unusual genre. *The Butcher of Abbeville* is in some ways a representative *fabliau* with its emphasis on sex and trickery and its low view of human nature (the people in the story will apparently do anything in return for a reward). It is also very characteristic that the priest, who ought to be celibate and charitable to strangers, is depicted as lecherous and materialistic and turns out to be the chief victim of the story.

Plot summary of *The Butcher of Abbeville*

The butcher of Abbeville, returning home from a fruitless journey to the market at Oisemont, asks lodging for the night from the priest of Bailleul. The priest rudely refuses him shelter. On the way out of town he comes upon the priest's sheepfold. The butcher steals one of the sheep and returns to the priest's house, offering to share the meat in return for lodging. The priest agrees, and he and his beautiful mistress enjoy the lamb roast with their guest. When it is time to go to sleep the butcher persuades the priest's serving maid to share his bed in return for the sheepskin. In the morning he finds the priest's mistress alone, and seduces her in return for the promise of the same sheepskin. Well-refreshed he then goes to the church to thank the priest and sells him the sheepskin, which he has left at his house. When he returns home the priest finds his mistress and his serving maid quarrelling over the ownership of the sheepskin he thinks he has just bought.

Then his shepherd, who has come to tell him that one of the sheep has been stolen, recognizes the sheepskin. The teller concludes by inviting the audience to debate who has most right to the sheepskin.

French text in W. Noomen and N. van den Boogaard eds. *Nouveau Receuil Complet des Fabliaux* (Assen, 1982), vol. 3; translation in R. Hellman and R. O'Gorman, *Fabliaux* (London, 1965), pp. 31–44.

Plot summary of *Heile of Beersele*

This is a Flemish *fabliau*, roughly contemporary with *The Miller's Tale*, which combines the same three elements (the misdirected kiss, the second flood, and the branding) to make a somewhat different story. Even if the two stories share a common source, which seems likely, their differences suggest that both poets imposed their own shape on the material as well as (in Chaucer's case) developing character, themes and dialogue. The Flemish version well illustrates the spirit of *fabliau*, while a comparison of the two can reveal how Chaucer adapted the inherited genre to his own purposes.

An Antwerp prostitute named Heile of Beersele once agreed to receive three clients the same night. She arranged for William the Miller to arrive in the early evening, the priest when the sleep-bell rang, and her neighbour the blacksmith at the time of the final curfew. William enjoyed her until the sleep-bell. When the priest arrived she told William to hide in a trough hanging in the rafters. After she and the priest had made love three times, he started to preach to her about a second flood coming to purge the world of its wickedness. When the blacksmith arrived Heile sent him away, saying that she was ill. He was disappointed and begged for a kiss at least. At Heile's suggestion, the priest stuck his bottom out of the window to receive the kiss. When the blacksmith realized the trick that had been played on him, he went to his forge and heated an iron rod. When he returned to the house to beg another kiss, the priest repeated his trick and was rewarded with a scalded bottom. He cried out for water which made William think the second flood had come. He cut his trough down from the rafters, fell to the floor and broke his arm. Running away from William, whom he thought was the devil, the priest fell into the cess-pit and was mocked by the neighbours. The story is told as a warning to those who associate with prostitutes.

Flemish text and English translation in W.F. Bryan and G. Dempster (eds.) *Sources and Analogues of Chaucer's Canterbury Tales* (Chicago, 1941), pp. 112–18.